John F. Kennedy

John F. Kennedy

Howard S. Kaplan

DK Publishing, Inc.

LONDON, NEW YORK, MELBOURNE,
MUNICH, AND DELHI

Designed for DK Publishing, Inc.
by Mark Johnson Davies

Series Editor : Beth Sutinis

Editorial Assistant : Madeline Farbman

Art Director : Dirk Kaufman

Publisher : Chuck Lang

Creative Director : Tina Vaughan

Photo Research : Tracy Armstead

Production : Chris Avgherinos

DTP Designer : Milos Orlovic

First American Edition, 2004
Published in the United States
by DK Publishing, Inc.
375 Hudson St., New York, New York 10014

04 05 06 07 08 10 9 8 7 6 5 4 3 2 1

Library of Congress Cataloging-in-Publication Data

Kaplan, Howard S. (Howard Stephen) [date]
DK biography: John F. Kennedy/written by Howard S. Kaplan.--
1st American ed.
p. cm. -- (DK biography)
Includes bibliographical references and index.
ISBN: 0-7566-0340-4 (PB) ISBN: 0-7566-0489-3 (HC)
1. Kennedy, John F. (John Fitzgerald), 1917-1963--Juvenile
literature. 2. Presidents--United States--Biography--Juvenile
literature. I. Title: John F. Kennedy. II. Title. III. Series.
E842.Z9K37 2004
973.922'092--dc22   2004007982

Color reproduction by GRB Editrice s.r.l., Italy
Printed and bound in China
by South China Printing Co., Ltd.

Discover more at
www.dk.com

Contents

November 22, 1963

The November day begins like any other: alarm clocks, coffee cups, school buses, and classroom bells. The milkman delivers his cold glass bottles of sweet cream and milk, while newspapers hit front doors with a familiar *thwack*. A man and a woman traveled yesterday from Washington, D.C., to Houston, Texas. Today they fly from Houston to a place called Love Field, outside of Dallas.

The day begins like any other day. The man and the woman get off the plane and are greeted by photographers. *Click.*

They are the most photographed couple in the world.
Click. She is handed red roses and adjusts her pink hat.
Click. Click. Click. The car is waiting—a convertible.
They take their place in the backseat and head downtown,
waving, smiling. The crowds can't get enough. The car
turns a corner. It moves slowly.

We want to shout at them to turn around, or pick
another car, or go down a different street. But we can't.
They drive straight into history.

chapter 1

You Don't Know Jack

Jack is burning. He's only two and a half. His cheeks are flushed red and his throat is so sore that it hurts when he swallows, his head aches, and his thin body is warm to the touch. *101 degrees.* The rash is spreading and leaves his skin as rough as sandpaper. There is nothing more contagious than scarlet fever. *102 degrees.* The mercury in the glass thermometer inches up; his temperature rises. *104 degrees.*

Outside it's winter and the gray sky is as drab as hospital sheets, but inside it's burning. It is February 20, 1920.

Penicillin, the miracle drug, has not been invented yet. It's not safe for Jack's mother, Rose, to take care of him because she's only hours away from giving birth to her fourth child, a girl they'll name Kathleen. As Rose would soon note on one of many plain index cards she kept to record and track her children's life experiences,

Baby Jack plays
on the beach.

her household was plunged into a state of "frantic terror" because her son was a "very, very sick little boy."

Jack's father Joe must do something, but there's not a hospital around that will take the boy. Scarlet fever is everywhere. Six hundred children in the Boston area are suffering from the disease, and there are only 125 beds at Boston's City Hospital. You do the math. But the Kennedys live outside of Boston, in Brookline, and are not eligible for a bed, even if one were available. Jack's fever rises.

Joe is frantic and calls upon his father-in-law, the sick boy's namesake, John "Honey Fitz" Fitzgerald, the former mayor of Boston, to help. He does, and Jack is given a bed. This is what money and position and power can do for you. It can put you on the right path; it can help you in your career; it can even save your life. Joe gets the best physician in the country, Harvard-trained Dr. Edwin Place, to look after his son.

Jack remains in the hospital for two months, and his father visits him almost daily. Each morning Joseph Kennedy wakes up early and goes to church to pray for his son. He makes a promise that if the boy recovers, he'll donate half of what he's worth to charity. After work he hurries to the hospital to be with Jack.

After two months in the hospital Jack is released, but he is sent to the Mansion House in Poland Springs, Maine, to recuperate in the fresh air for two weeks. Joe keeps his promise and writes out a check for $3,700 to the Guild of St. Apollonia, an organization of Catholic dentists who provide dental care to needy children.

It's now May, three months since the fever raged. Jack is cured, but his childhood will be marked by disease: whooping cough, chicken pox, ear infections. You name it, Jack gets it. His mother records his illnesses on one of her index cards. It will fill up quickly.

His family will joke about the risk a mosquito takes in biting *him*.

———————— • ————————

Picture this: Your ancestors have lived on the same farm for years, but now something is going terribly wrong. You live in Ireland, the greenest place on earth; you have a farm and live off the land, but now the land turns on you. The one crop that has sustained your family for generations, the potato, is being wiped out. A fungus, white and fuzzy, kills the plant and spreads from farm to farm faster than gossip. Rain helps the bacteria grow and spread. The newspapers call it a blight and then a plague. You can dig and dig and dig and come up with nothing but potatoes that look like black stones. People starve. They riot for food. Some collapse on the way to the poorhouse. The famine not only takes lives, it ultimately wins. Some will choose to stay, and others will leave for America.

Between 1845 and 1850 nearly one million people died of famine and disease because of the potato famine. Emigration to America was one answer, but it was hardly a cure. The ships that sailed from Ireland to the U.S. were known as "coffin ships" because of the high death rate of the passengers onboard. It is estimated that 4,500,000 Irish people came to America between 1820 and 1860. At least 500,000 of those Irish arrived in America during the famine years.

Imagine that you are the great-grandchild of people who struggled across oceans, lost loved ones to disease, and

Life During the Irish Potato Famine

Farmers in Ireland at the time of the potato famine lived in very poor conditions. Most did not own the land they farmed. It was often rented from landlords, most of whom were British or Protestant and treated the mainly Catholic peasants as inferior people. The farmers paid their rent to the landlords in crops and would live off the excess they could produce. If they did not produce enough to pay off the landlords, they were threatened with being evicted— thrown off—their land. Once evicted, the peasants had little choice but to go to a poorhouse for charity or to leave Ireland.

withstood life in slums so that their children would have a better chance at life.

Then, when those ancestors get to America, they have to fight prejudice because Irish Catholics are not always welcome. John Fitzgerald Kennedy will learn about all this when he gets older: He will even travel to Ireland to seek out relatives. He is the great-grandson of strong-willed people: It is in his blood.

Boston in the middle of the nineteenth century feels more like two cities than one. Society's elite were called the Boston Brahmins—Brahmin being the term for members of the

Like many immigrants, Jack's great grandparents came to the United States on crowded ships.

highest level of Hindu society in India. Many of the Boston Brahmins came over on the *Mayflower*. In contrast, a few hundred years later, the

Kennedys and the Fitzgeralds and the new immigrant Irish traveled on coffin ships. The Brahmins live in elegant townhouses, while on the other side of town the Irish barely get by in cramped apartment buildings called tenements. Poverty, disease, and overcrowding are with them constantly.

Jack's paternal great-grandfather, Patrick Kennedy, settles in East Boston and works as a cooper, making and repairing wooden casks. He marries Bridget Murphy, has three daughters and one son, and dies of cholera in 1858 at age 35. The son, Patrick Joseph, is just 10 months old when his father passes away. P.J., as he is called, grows up and prospers. He starts a liquor importing business, and, in 1887, P.J. marries Mary Augusta Hickey, the daughter of another prosperous businessman. P.J. becomes active in local Democratic Party politics. Mary and P.J. have only one child who survives: a son, Joseph Patrick Kennedy.

Thomas Fitzgerald arrives in the United States in 1854, settles in Boston's North End, and marries Rosanna Cox in 1857. He makes his money as a street peddler, saves up enough to purchase a grocery store, then buys tenement buildings and rents them out to Irish laborers. This is what is known as the American dream. His son, John Francis Fitzgerald,

is born on February 12, 1863, and is baptized at St. Stephen's Church, the spiritual center of the Irish Catholic community. Unlike

> ### "SWEET ADELINE"
> Written in 1903 by Richard Gerard, "Sweet Adeline" was a popular song performed by barbershop quartets.

many of the children born into these hard times, John Francis lives. Not only that; he thrives.

See John run: He is the fastest boy in the North End, and he never stops running. He attends the prestigious Boston Latin School where famous men such as the writers Henry David Thoreau, Ralph Waldo Emerson, and Henry James studied. Then he attends Harvard Medical School but drops out to look after his siblings after his father's death in 1885. He begins to work for the local political boss in the North End, Matthew Keany. Keany takes him under his wing, and John Fitzgerald's life in politics begins.

See John run for office: Rising in local ward politics, he would go on to serve in the Massachusetts State Senate, and in 1895 was

Jack's grandfathers, Honey Fitz and P.J., go for a ride in 1911. The two knew each other from Boston political circles.

elected from the Ninth Congressional District to the U.S. House of Representatives, a seat his grandson Jack would hold about fifty years later. In 1906, Fitzgerald would become mayor of Boston.

> *"Honey Fitz can talk you blind, on any subject you can find."*
>
> A popular verse of the time, commenting on Honey Fitz's way with words

Rose, born in 1890, was her father's favorite, and since her mother, Josie Hannon, shied away from public functions, Rose was often at her father's side as his hostess. Rose called her father a "natural performer" noting that "the political arena was his stage." Rose, who was fluent in French and German, often accompanied her father on his political outings. She became his "companion, hostess, and assistant on a good many of the trips he took."

He gets his nickname "Honey Fitz" from the honey-sweet way he sings his favorite song, "Sweet Adeline," often while standing on a table. Compact in size, he's also known as the "Little General."

———— • ————

People are born; families are made. It seems as if Joe and Rose were destined to be together. They meet as children—he's seven and she's five—at Old Orchard Beach, Maine, a place many Boston Irish Catholics visit for vacation during the summer. Ten summers after the first meeting, they would be devoted to one another.

On October 7, 1914, Rose married Joseph P. Kennedy.

Rose, a graduate of Dorchester High School in Boston, was also educated at Sacred Heart convents in Boston and abroad. Schools run by Roman Catholic nuns and priests, and where, often, the students live away from home, are called convent schools. Rose's father had promised to send her to Wellesley, a respected women's college, after high school but then went back on his word, leaving her heartbroken.

Joe's a Harvard man and goes into banking at the Columbia Trust Company, a bank his father, P.J. Kennedy, helped found in East Boston. At 25, Joe becomes the youngest bank president in the country, and, according to Rose, "probably the world." Joe and Rose marry in October of 1914 and set up house in Brookline, Massachusetts.

Here's the family's first house on Beals Street. It's wooden and green and when you walk in you'll find seven rooms, plus two maids' rooms in the attic. The parlor, dining room, and kitchen were on the ground floor.

Old Orchard Beach, Maine, was a favorite vacation spot for Boston's wealthy "High Irish" families. Rose is second from left and Joe is second from right.

On the second floor is a bedroom for Joe and Rose, and a nursery for the children. If you visit the house today, you can still see the bassinet that held all nine children, one after the other.

By trolley, it took about a half-hour to get into the bustling city of Boston. Not a bad commute by anyone's standard.

John F. Kennedy was born in this house on Beals Street in Brookline, Massachusetts.

Rose filled the living room, or parlor, as it was called in those days, with prints of the great artworks she had seen in Europe during her travels and studies abroad.

They received an Ivers and Ponds grand piano from her uncles as a wedding present, as well as cups and saucers "blazoned with shamrocks" from family friend Sir Thomas Lipton, a famous yachtsman who made a name for himself in the tea business.

When it comes to raising their young children, Joe will treat his family like a well-run business, while Rose concerns herself with religion and the daily lives of the young Kennedys.

17

chapter 2

Jack the Elf

Jack is a reader. He loves books, and his favorites are the tales of Billy Whiskers, a goat who has "kids"; and *The Adventures of Reddy Fox* by Thornton Burgess. His mother, Rose, says that he has a "strong romantic and idealistic streak." The books he likes have "flair, action, and color." You are what you read, perhaps.

Jack is a dreamer. He comes late to meals. Maybe he's somewhere by himself with a favorite book. The rule of the house is: If you're late to the dinner table, you cannot eat what's been served previously.

So if you arrive for dessert,

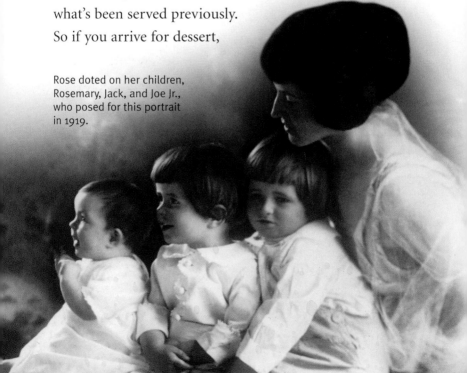

Rose doted on her children, Rosemary, Jack, and Joe Jr., who posed for this portrait in 1919.

dessert is all you get. But Jack is so thin and has been so sick that when he comes late to the table, misses another meal, and disappears into the kitchen to have the cook serve him some food on the sly (hopefully with a lot of rich, fatty gravy), Rose looks the other way.

Jack is a dreamer and a reader. When it comes time to think of the perfect present for her son, Rose thinks of a "storybook with large colorful pictures." When he's older, Jack moves on to the Waverly novels of Sir Walter Scott and to the tales of King Arthur and the Round Table. Rose thinks that when he's doing his math homework or picking his clothes up off the floor, he's not really paying attention to the task at hand; instead he's in some far-off land, "weaving daydreams." Perhaps it's a story of King Arthur and his knights and Jack is wondering what it would be like to be a hero, a leader of men: what it would be like to live in Camelot.

Rose looks at her son Jack and this is what she sees: a narrow face and ears that stick out a bit, and his hair—well, that seems to have a life of its own. Jack's appearance reminds Rose of an elf, "a very lively elf" who, when he isn't ill, is charming and energetic. He has his own way of doing things, saying things, and is really not like anybody else.

Then again, Rose is not your typical mother. After all, she was the daughter of Boston's mayor, one of the most colorful leaders to hold office in a long time. There's plenty going on at home and Rose likes to have a room for herself where she can just be Rose, away from running a household that will total nine children plus maids, a nanny, chauffeur, and a cook. Years later, on the family's property in Hyannis Port, Massachusetts, she'll have a little separate place of her own. The kids will affectionately nickname it "the White House."

Young Jack, dressed as a policeman, assumes an air of authority.

But now, even as a young mother, Rose loves to travel. She has an independent spirit of adventure. Later in life, Jack will respond to qualities like these when he chooses his own wife.

But for now, Jack is five, and he sees his mother packing her bags to take a trip with Aunt Agnes, her sister. He's not too happy about this. Joe Sr. has agreed that Rose can travel as she wishes and that he will be home to attend to the children when she's gone. This trip will take her out west for

six weeks—a long time for a child to be without his mother, especially one like Jack who has been so sick.

"Gee," Jack looks up at his mother and says, "you're a great mother to go away and leave your children alone."

Rose feels guilty and leaves the house with a heavy heart, so she sneaks back to the porch and looks into the window. She sees Jack laughing and looking like he's having a good time and is convinced that he has already forgotten about his words to her. He will be lonely while his mother is away, though the house, in typical Kennedy fashion, is filling with people.

Joe and Rose aboard the SS *Aquitania*, coming home from Europe.

Soon the sound of an automobile pulling up to the house will be heard and Rose's father, Grandpa Fitz, will come and take the children out: to historic Boston sites, to baseball games at Fenway Park, and to the Boston Public Gardens where Jack loves to ride the boats that are shaped like swans.

Jack and his older brother, Joseph P. Kennedy, Jr., are like a lot of brothers: they can't live with each

other and they can't live without each other. As young boys Joe Jr. and Jack get into mischief: They steal false mustaches from a shop; when they go to a restaurant that has the sign NO DOGS ALLOWED on the door, they add the word HOT in front of DOGS; they invent a song about bedbugs and cooties; and, most painfully, they form a club where they initiate new members by sticking them with pins.

But as they get older the camaraderie gets mixed with competition and jealousy, and they will often come to blows, sometimes violently. Joe Jr. is the neat one, the one who hangs up his clothes at the end of the day, the one who cares about his appearance. Sometimes Jack looks rumpled; his clothes hang off of him. Their mother Rose dressed them in identical sailor suits—the fashion of the time. But underneath their similar clothing, the boys are becoming different people.

Fenway Park, where the Boston Red Sox have played since 1912, is the oldest Major League Baseball field in use today.

Joe Jr. has a quick temper. Jack is more easy going. One day they decide to have a bicycle race and start by going around the block in opposite directions to see who can return home first.

Ready…set…go! They're off, feet pumping and spoked wheels spinning so fast they blur. They round the last corner at around the same time and ride toward each other head-on. One of them needs to get out of the way, but Joe isn't flinching, and what Jack lacks in muscle he's gaining in guts. Neither boy yields, so they crash right into each other. Joe Jr. stands up, brushes himself off, and walks away without a scratch. Jack needs twenty-eight stitches to put him back together again.

They will keep fighting. And Jack will always be a few steps behind Joe—never as good in the schoolroom or on the athletic field.

Despite their differences, Joe Sr. wants his sons to be close. Crossing to England on the *Normandie* in 1935, Joe Sr. summons Jack to his side to meet Lawrence Fisher, one of the seven famous Fisher brothers of the General Motors Corporation. "Jack," his father tells him, "…I wanted you to see what success brothers have who stick together."

Blood is thicker than water, and Joe Sr. wants Kennedy blood to be the thickest brew on the block.

Rose believes in discipline and spanks her children now and then. She keeps a ruler in a desk, but a nearby hanger will do the trick, too. She's not cruel, but she believes in giving a whack now and then. If Joe Jr. or Jack were the object of her anger, they might take their cue from Hans and Fritz,

Rose's Card File

Rose was a very well-organized mother, and she always kept track of her children's health. This card file had notes about all of the children's doctor visits, illnesses, and weight. Because Jack had so many medical problems, his file was very long. Rose learned this habit from her father, Honey Fitz, who kept a card file to keep track of political deals.

the Katzenjammer Kids, rebellious twins from the Sunday comics who stuffed their pants with a pillow when a spanking was coming. Rose, of course, could see what they had done, but sometimes would let the boys get away with it.

Joe Sr. would never spank his children, but he had a way of looking at them, casting his steel blue eyes into "Daddy's look." That seemed to do the trick. When the children were misbehaving he'd say firmly, "cut out the applesauce" or knock off "the monkey business."

Rose and Joe Sr. think that at mealtime the children should share their views on world and national events and learn how to be good talkers and good listeners. Rose clips articles out of the newspaper and pins them to the bulletin board. The children—those old enough to read—are supposed to take a look at the board and develop opinions to share at dinner.

Rose was also fond of taking outings with her young family while Joe was off on business trips. She takes the family around Brookline—often to the five-and-dime at Coolidge's Corner—and then to various parts of Boston so that she can show them sites important to United States history. They visit Bunker Hill, Plymouth Rock, and the Old North Church—the site of Paul Revere's signal that the British were coming. Rose takes them to Boston Harbor and weaves a tale of the Boston Tea Party.

With her family ever-growing, Rose becomes grateful for zippers. Before zippers, almost all clothing was fastened with buttons. Whenever the family went out in the winter in their buttoned leggings, there were hours spent buttoning, and

"Of those to whom much is given, much will be required."

St. Luke, as recited to JFK by his mother, Rose

Jack and Joe were often dressed in matching outfits. Here they wear collars and hats that remind one of pilgrims.

unbuttoning the buttons, then fastening the buttons that had loosened, dangled, and would have been lost for good. Sewing on buttons was one job Rose liked doing herself.

Rose is always looking for new experiences to share with her children. One day she decides to take the children out blueberry picking; wild blueberries could be found on most parts of Cape Cod. So she loads her five children into the car, travels over bumpy, sandy roads with her brood screaming and laughing, until she spies a huge patch of berries and wildflowers just ripe for the picking. Each child gets a little tin pail and heads out.

It's a perfect day until Eunice gets stung by a bee and starts to scream. The other children panic. Then Jack comes bounding up screaming, with arms waving. *Ants!* Jack sat on an anthill. He is now covered in ants. His clothes are frantically torn off and are shaken out. Rose packs up the kids in the car and heads

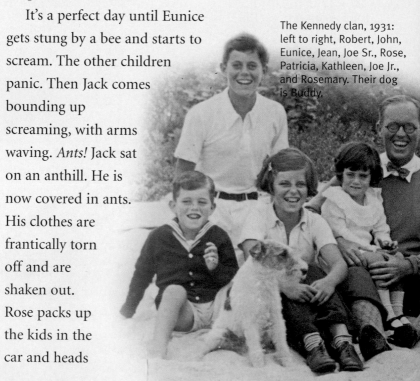
The Kennedy clan, 1931: left to right, Robert, John, Eunice, Jean, Joe Sr., Rose, Patricia, Kathleen, Joe Jr., and Rosemary. Their dog is Buddy.

home, stopping at the local market to buy three quarts of
blueberries. She never mentions blueberry picking again.

Rose and Joe's family will gradually grow to include
nine children. The first group of children includes Joseph
"Joe" Jr., born in 1915; John, called "Jack," born in 1917;
Rosemary, born in 1918; and Kathleen, who goes by the
nickname "Kick," is born in 1920. Eunice follows shortly after
in 1921; then Patricia is born in 1924; Robert, known as
"Bobby," is born in 1925; then Jean comes along in 1928.
Finally, Edward, the youngest, arrives in 1932. Most people
know him as "Teddy."

Joe has to be in New York on business when Patricia is
born. He returns to Boston about two weeks after her birth
and finds his five older children—
ranging in age from two to ten—
waiting anxiously for him at
the train station, yelling,
"Daddy, daddy, we've got
another baby…." Joe greets
them with open arms
while he spies the faces of
the other passengers. He
imagines they must be
thinking: "What that
fellow there certainly
doesn't need right now
is another baby."

27

chapter **3**

Jack at School

Jack and Joe bound out of the house for Devotion, a public
school named after Edward Devotion, son of a seventeenth-
century French-Huguenot settler in Brookline. The best part is
that the school is only a few blocks from their new house on
Naples Road. It's October 1921, and Jack is four years old.

After school the boys have too much time on their hands
and get into all kinds of trouble. One day Joe makes his way
to the roof of a neighbor's garage. On another day, Jack
climbs out the bathroom window and is discovered on the
roof of his own house, thirty feet above the ground.

A few years later, when one of Jack's teachers is due at the
house to report on Jack's behavior at school, he tells his
parents, "You know I am getting on all right and if you study
too much, you're liable to go crazy."

Though Rose is a fan of public schools, where her boys
could meet the sons of grocers and plumbers, she and Joe
move the boys from Devotion to Dexter, a private school
where the day begins at 8:15 AM and ends at 4:45 PM. In the
school uniform of short pants, stockings, and a red sweater,
Joe Jr. and Jack dash off to class.

The morning sessions are devoted to academics, while the
afternoons are filled with athletics, and both boys make the
football team. In the fourth grade, Jack becomes captain and

quarterback, and before an important game receives a telegram from his father addressed to Captain Jack Kennedy. Looks like Jack has scored a touchdown with his father.

At the Dexter School, Joe (in square) got better grades, but some teachers thought Jack (in circle) was smarter.

The school's dual focus of brains and brawn appeals to Joe Sr. That, plus the fact that his boys would now mingle with the privileged children of Boston's wealthy elite, which is something Joe never had even though he attended the Boston Latin School and Harvard. He was never accepted into the Boston Brahmin society, and he wanted his children to avoid the prejudices he felt as an Irish Catholic in a city run by Protestants.

Jack was a fierce competitor as a defenseman on his school's football team.

All is not rosy, however, for Joe Jr. and Jack. Jack feels that he and his brother are probably the only Catholics around. They are called names sometimes, and get into fights.

In 1927, Joe Sr. makes the decision to move his family to New York, partly to be closer to the Wall Street hub, and partly to make his trips out to Hollywood a little easier. He's become a film producer in the growing movie business, working, most famously, with actress Gloria Swanson. (Swanson is a silent film actress who is trying to make the move to "talkies"—movies with sound.) Joe has the knack of being in the right place at the right time. Because of his many business successes, President Franklin D. Roosevelt will make him the chairman of the new Securities and Exchange Commission in 1932. By the time of Joe's death in 1969, he will be estimated to be worth half a billion dollars. The term "mover and shaker" fits Joe Sr. like a glove.

Making the move from Massachusetts to New York allows Joe to put behind him the anti-Irish Catholic prejudice that plagued him at Harvard when he couldn't break into the popular groups or when he was refused membership at the Cohasset Golf Club on the South Shore, 20 miles from Boston.

Before leaving for New York, Joe Sr. buys a house on Cape Cod at Hyannis Port, so the family will always have a home in Massachusetts. Then he rents a private railroad car and the Kennedys, whose ancestors left Ireland on coffin ships, now head to the next chapter of their lives in luxury. Joe Sr. buys an estate in Bronxville, a wealthy suburb of New York City.

Joe Jr. and Jack attend the Riverdale Country Day School for a few years where Jack is an okay student, keeping a steady B minus average. A few years later, Joe Jr. is sent to the exclusive Choate School, but when it's Jack's time to go, Rose steps in and chooses Canterbury Prep, where Jack would receive a Catholic education. Both schools are in Connecticut.

CANTERBURY SCHOOL
NEW MILFORD, CONNECTICUT

Record of John Kennedy, Form II

From November 1 to December 6, 1930.

Any average from 90% to 100% is accounted "Very Good"; from 80% to 90% "Good"; from 70% to 80% "Fair"; from 60% to 70% "Poor"; and below 60% "Unsatisfactory".

SUBJECT	DAILY WORK	EFFORT AND APPLICATION	FORM AVERAGE
English II	86	Good	71.69
Latin II	55	Poor	64.35
History II	77	Good	67.00
Mathematics II	95	Good	61.69
Science II	72	Good	66.62
Religion II	75	Fair	78.46
AVERAGE: 77.00			

This report is not quite so good as the last one. The damage was done chiefly by "Poor" effort in Latin, in which Jack got a mark of 55. He can do better than this. In fact, his average should be well in the 80's.

N.H.

Most students in Jack's day had to take Latin. This report card shows it was Jack's worst subject.

Joe Jr., the favorite son and the rising star of the Kennedy family, has a tough time adjusting to boarding school. His grades suffer, and for the first time in his life, his golden boy image is tarnished. When Joe Jr. is caught playing rough in the halls by senior classmates (known as sixth formers), they paddle and swat him hard enough to raise blisters on his backside. Jack lights up when he hears about his brother's paddling and writes to his father, "What I wouldn't have given to be a sixth former."

But first, Jack will have to get through a year at Canterbury, which he barely does because he has to withdraw due to illness before the term ends.

By the time Jack walks onto the campus at Choate, a thin willow of a boy among the sturdy elms, in the fall of 1931, Joe Jr. has not only found his stride, but he's looking like one of the best student-athletes the school has ever seen. Headmaster George St. John praises him to the hilt— probably enough to make Jack want to pack up and go home. Before Jack arrives, Rose writes to the headmaster, thanking him for all he has done for Joe Jr., and also to let him know that Jack is "quite different from Joe."

For one thing, Jack is still a slob. His dorm room is notorious for its mess, and Mr. Maher, the housemaster, is livid. Joe Sr. frequently calls Jack out for his sloppiness and disregard for finances or any kind of responsibility. He tells Jack that he received a bill for $10.80 for one month of suit pressing (an enormous sum at the time), and that is way too much.

Choate Preparatory School, founded in 1890, is one of the most prestigious secondary schools in the U.S.

If only Jack would learn to pick up after himself and stop leaving his clothes piled on the floor, then all that laundering wouldn't be necessary. It's not the money Joe cares about; it's his son's poor habits that he wants changed.

But Jack's like that academically as well: a little sloppy and a little careless. His father is worried that he's not living up to his potential and that all the trappings of the Kennedy wealth have spoiled him.

Rose writes to the headmaster's wife, Mrs. St. John, about Jack's health: Is he eating enough? Rose says he only weighs "$114^{1/2}$–115…after supper." He has problems with fallen arches, so can you look out for him and make sure he gets better shoes? Oh, and about his knee…And so it goes.

Jack remains, however, quite mischievous, and suffers the consequences when caught. Rose sends him a crate of oranges from Florida, and Jack takes to pelting them out his window at passing friends. *Demerit!* He fills a fellow student's room from floor to ceiling with all the pillows from the dorm.

DEMERIT

A mark against one's record that can result in a loss of privileges for the offender.

Demerit! Perhaps this is how Jack gets the attention that comes so naturally to his older brother. Upon graduating, Joe Jr. wins the

esteemed Harvard prize, given to the most academically and athletically gifted senior. The day of the award ceremony is not a happy one for Jack, who watches his parents lavish love and respect on Joe Jr. Jack knows he's "got the goods," but he just can't deliver them yet.

Jack never really needs help in getting into trouble; soon, though, he has a devoted partner in crime.

With Joe Jr. gone, Jack meets his best—and lifelong—friend, Kirk LeMoyne Billings, or "Lem," while working on the school yearbook, *The Brief.* The pair, plus friends Rip and Butch, form the Muckers Club and stir up trouble—"muckers" being the word Headmaster St. John uses for

Jack graduated from Choate in 1935.

troublemakers. Jack and Lem are drawn to each other. It is easy to want to be around Jack, whose smile has enough wattage to light the entire campus, but the boys have another bond—both have older, successful brothers in whose golden footprints they don't want to walk.

Jack says the muckers like to "buck the system." He and his friends have membership charms made up: golden shovels with the words CHOATE MUCKERS CLUB engraved on them. Headmaster St. John is not amused and threatens to expel them.

When this only seems to egg Jack on, Joe Sr. is called away from his high-level job as the chairman of the Securities and Exchange Commission for a talk about the situation. Jack sweats it out and promises to disband the club, realizing that what he was really doing was mucking up his life. He pulls himself together so that his last year at Choate—his year as a sixth former—is muck-free.

Despite less than stellar grades—graduating slightly below the middle of the class—Jack is voted most likely to succeed from the class of 1935. Jack decides he wants to go to Princeton with Lem and his friends, even though his father wants him to attend Harvard.

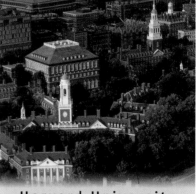

Harvard University

When Harvard University was founded in 1636, it shared the philosophy of the Puritans who had come to America sixteen years earlier. The Puritans believed in leading simple lives dictated by the teachings of the Protestant church. For many years, most Harvard students were wealthy Protestant men. When Joe Sr. attended Harvard in 1908, he was one of few Catholics. But being different made him even more determined to succeed.

Jack travels to England with his sister Kick and his parents. His goal is to spend one year studying at the London School of Economics, just as Joe had done, before college. But Jack falls ill and has to drop out after one month.

Back home, Jack convinces his father to let him attend

Princeton University. But after two hepatitis flare-ups he has to leave school. Jack goes out west to Arizona to recover; he has asthma, too.

When he's healed, he decides that rather than return to Princeton, it's time to wear the crimson, and he enters Harvard.

Freshman Jack Kennedy walks though the gates of Harvard Yard in the fall of 1936 and heads toward his room at Wheldon Hall. As at Choate, his older brother has gotten there first and is a distinguished member of the student body. Unlike Joe, who always seems to win, Jack runs for student council and loses. In sports, his low weight and lanky frame keep him from succeeding in football; one good tackle during his sophomore year ruptures a spinal disc, ending his days on the gridiron. He almost makes the varsity swimming team in the backstroke, but a case of influenza sends him to the hospital. His roommate, Torbert "Torby" Macdonald, sneaks steaks and malteds into the infirmary, then sneaks Jack out to the pool so he can practice his backstroke. The day of the race, Jack loses the time trial by a few seconds.

In the summer of 1937, between Jack's freshman and sophomore years, he and Lem Billings travel around Europe on the cheap, as Lem has very little money.

In London, shortly after being appointed ambassador, Joe steps out with his sons, Jack and Joe Jr.

Nazis cross the Cologne Bridge during Germany's invasion of the Rhineland in 1936. This act of aggression threw the nations of Europe into conflict.

Overseas, Jack sees the world from a new perspective. That fall, President Franklin Delano Roosevelt names Joe Sr. the Ambassador to the Court of St. James in England, a first for an Irish-American. Inside the embassy all is well. But outside, the air is thick with rumors of war and Hitler's plan for the *Anschluss*, the takeover of Austria by Germany. Then the Munich Agreement, the Pact that gave a part of Czechoslovakia to Germany to satisfy an old claim, is broken when the Germans invade the rest of Czechoslovakia. English Prime Minister Neville Chamberlain wants "peace at any price," and other European leaders agree to try to avoid war with Germany. Joe Sr. writes to F.D.R. and says that the U.S. should not get involved in the conflict. Having this view will eventually cost him his job.

For a politician in the making, Jack is in the right place at the right time. When the Nazis torpedo the British ocean liner *Athenia*, with 300 Americans on board, Ambassador Joe sends Jack to Glasgow, Scotland, to interview the survivors.

In time, all the Kennedy children come to London to live and go to school. Jack spends the first semester of junior year at Harvard and the second semester in England, with plans to graduate from college with the class of 1940. Jack proposes a senior thesis about Britain not being prepared for war.

His proposal approved, he then goes on a fact-finding tour of Eastern Europe. He travels to Poland, Russia, and then Palestine in the Middle East, and, thanks to Ambassador Kennedy's influence, he gets into Nazi-occupied Prague, Czechoslovakia. Surely his thesis would benefit from all this research.

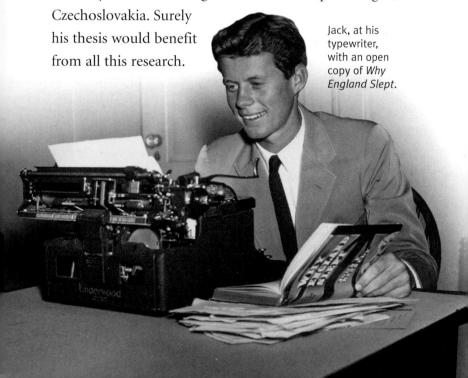

Jack, at his typewriter, with an open copy of *Why England Slept*.

Peace in Our Time?

Europe was hit hard by World War I, and the Allies—Britain, Italy, France, and the U.S.— had demanded harsh terms of surrender from Germany. Angered at their treatment and under the control of a new military government led by Adolf Hitler, Germany invaded Austria in 1938. France and England took no action. When Hitler demanded part of Czechoslovakia, British Prime Minister Neville Chamberlain arranged for Germany to have this land if Hitler made no more claims. Chamberlain announced that there would be "peace in our time," but he was wrong. Six months later, Germany invaded the rest of Czechoslovakia.

European territorial boundaries in 1941

Axis Forces   Allied Forces   Neutrals

Germany invades Poland on September 1, 1939, and two days later England declares war on Germany. Jack puts on his double-breasted pinstripe suit and, with Kick and Joe Jr., goes to listen to Chamberlain speak in the House of Commons.

Jack's thesis, "Appeasement at Munich," earns high honors. Jack decides to publish it as a book with the title *Why England Slept.* The title deliberately echoes new British Prime Minister Winston Churchill's own book *While England Slept,* which called for a strong response to the aggressive Nazi government in Germany. When Jack's book hits the best-seller lists and sells more than 40,000 copies, he becomes something of a celebrity.

chapter 4

War Breaks Out

The Kennedy children grow up wealthy. They have three impressive homes and a flurry of domestic help to keep everything running smoothly. The Great Depression, the period between 1929 and the early 1940s when America's economy collapsed, didn't really register on the Kennedy scale; in fact, Joe Sr.'s wealth improved during those years because he was savvy enough to have gotten out of the stock market just in time. During the Depression, Jack confessed to his father that he hadn't heard about the stock market crash until months after it happened. Money was the means to Joe's ends: it would enable his children to rise in

After losing jobs in the Great Depression, many people depended on breadlines for food.

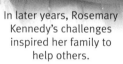

the social world, while allowing them—especially his boys—to devote their lives to public service.

Some people say Joe used insider trading to make money in the markets, others said he was a bootlegger during the age of Prohibition, when the sale and consumption of alcoholic beverages was illegal. Whatever the truth, Joe Kennedy was a shrewd businessman, at home in Hollywood, Wall Street, Washington, D.C., and the Court of St. James.

In later years, Rosemary Kennedy's challenges inspired her family to help others.

The oldest children, Joe Jr., Kathleen, and Jack—but not Rosemary, who is mentally handicapped—become a family unit of their own. In New York, their bedrooms are on the same floor, separated by a large game room. As young adults, they all attend private schools in Connecticut: the boys go to Choate and Kick goes to the Convent of the Sacred Heart. By all accounts they are smart, handsome, gifted, and move through life like yachts among rowboats: It is all smooth sailing. It seems as if nothing can change their lives, as if there is an invisible set of stairs designed for these three Kennedy children, and every day they ascend a little higher. It's not like that for Rosemary.

It sounds to us now like something out of a horror movie. You imagine a stainless steel laboratory, the mad doctor with the gleam in his eye, his white coat, the too-perfect hair, the

metal instruments. And the word—"lobotomy"—its three Os making the word sound like an extended moan.

Rosemary is becoming a woman physically, but mentally she remains a child. She is prone to violent fits and tantrums and is sometimes found wandering out alone late at night. She is out of control. Joe Sr. seeks help and is told about the wonder operation, the lobotomy. A sharp stab to the frontal lobe of the brain makes the patient forget the bad feelings. The goal of the lobotomy is to separate the girl from her problems. Joe

The U.S. at War

When war broke out in Europe, the United States was still coming out of the Depression that had followed World War I, and most Americans wanted to stay out of the new conflict. However, on December 7, 1941, Japanese planes attacked the naval base at Pearl Harbor in Hawaii, killing more than 2,000 people. The next day, the U.S. declared war against Japan.

Sr. arranges for the operation to take place in October 1941, but he doesn't tell Rose or any of the children.

The operation is a failure, and Rosemary, once called the most beautiful of the Kennedy girls, is permanently damaged. She can barely hold her head straight. For all purposes, she is gone. Her body remains, but she's just a shell now. Joe keeps quiet and arranges for her to be sent to a school for the

mentally disabled in Wisconsin, and Rose is told to stay away. In fact, it will take Rose more than twenty years to learn the truth about what Joe Sr. has done to their daughter.

—————— • ——————

In the spring of 1941, Joe Jr. senses America is going to become involved in the war, so after his second year at Harvard Law, he decides to volunteer for the Air Force. His training heats up after the Japanese attack Pearl Harbor on December 7, and he gets his wings in May of 1942. The following fall, Joe Jr. flies B-24s with the British Coastal Command.

Jack volunteers for the Army soon after his twenty-fourth birthday, but with his bad back, he fails the physical. He then goes out for the Navy, and, with his father pulling a few strings, passes the physical.

It must have been terrifying for Rose and Joe Sr. to watch their sons prepare for battle. In 1917, when idealistic young men went off to fight World War I and many never came back, Joe had held his little namesake in his arms and whispered to Rose, "This is the only happiness that lasts."

Jack doesn't ship out right away. He starts his duty

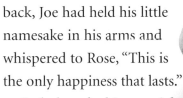

Jack and Joe Jr. in their naval uniforms.

John F. Kennedy, skipper of *PT-109*, on board his boat.

in Washington, D.C., at the Office of Naval Intelligence, then is sent to Charleston, South Carolina, then finally to Chicago for training before being called to sea. In the fall of 1942, Lieutenant John F. Kennedy is transferred to PT boats; early in 1943, he is shipped out to the South Pacific and becomes skipper— the officer in charge—of *PT-109*.

In April 1943, Jack finds himself on the island of Tulagi, in the Solomon Islands. *PT-109* is not in the best shape, and Jack and his crew clean it up to make it seaworthy.

In the early morning hours of August 2, 1943, the Japanese destroyer *Amagiri* rams straight into *PT-109* and slices it in two. Jack is thrown into the cockpit and slams his bad back. This is how it feels to die, Jack thinks to himself. Jack's men cling to debris to stay afloat. There is a burst of fire, and as part of the boat sinks, it tries to pull men down with it. The sea is a greasy strip of flaming gasoline. When Jack yells into the dark night for his men to call out where they are, two do not respond. Andrew Kirksey and Harold Marney had been killed on impact.

After hours in the water, and with *PT-109* sinking, Jack

SOUTH PACIFIC

The part of the world's largest ocean that is south of the Equator and includes thousands of tropical islands.

PT Boats

Patrol Torpedo boats were about eighty feet long and made out of plywood. Heavily armed and carrying a crew of about a dozen men, PT boats were designed to patrol the waters and fire on Japanese ships that were transporting military supplies. PT boats were the fastest boats in the U.S. Navy fleet. They could travel at a speed of up to 40 knots (nautical miles per hour).

spots a small island three miles in the distance. He decides he and his men should swim there. Jack tows Patrick McMahon, the most severely wounded man, by clenching the ties of his life jacket between his teeth. Hours later, all eleven men reach the island and collapse. Jack and his men have been in the water for more than fifteen hours. Though the men are safe, there's no food or drinkable water on the island. Jack swims through the Ferguson Passage in hopes of signaling a passing boat. But none are seen, and he returns to the small island.

Jack persuades his men to swim to another island, where there are coconuts.

Jack and a crew member then swim to Nauru Island, where they find food, as well as natives whom Jack asks for help. He carves the message "Nauru Isl native knows posit he can pilot 11 alive

In 2000, Hasbro toy company released an action figure of Lieutenant John F. Kennedy.

45

Jack's awards
for heroism

need small boat Kennedy" into a coconut shell and hands it to one of the natives, saying, "Rendova, Rendova," the name of an American military base. The following day, Jack and his crew are rescued.

When people ask Jack how he became a war hero, he replies, "It was involuntary. They sank my boat." For his heroism, Jack is awarded the Navy and Marine Corps Medal, and for injuries he received while saving his men, the Purple Heart.

Joe Jr. is fighting in the same war at the same time, but halfway around the world. The Germans, who had blasted London in the Battle of Britain, are now launching deadly V-1 strikes from the French coast. V-1 bombs are known as "doodlebugs," or buzz bombs, because of the sound they make. It's not the sound of the drone that's so scary, but the silence afterward. The pilot has fifteen seconds before the explosion.

Jack kept the coconut with the rescue message as a souvenir. It sat on his desk as a paperweight.

The Allies—the United States, Britain, and the countries who stand with them—need to get rid of bunkers where the Germans launch the V-1s. It's a deadly mission because the pilot needs to aim his plane, filled with explosives, right at the bunker, bailing out before impact.

Joe Jr. volunteers. Strapped

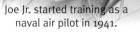

into the plane, Joe and his company of men are on target. They ascend to the proper altitude, make adjustments to instruments, and then the unthinkable happens—the plane blows up, killing Joe Jr. instantly.

Joe Jr. started training as a naval air pilot in 1941.

The Kennedys are home in Hyannis Port, when they get the news. It is after lunch when the Air Force chaplains arrive. Rose goes to wake her napping husband, and then they hear the news that their son has been lost in action. It's as if the wind has been punched out of them. It's not the sound of the words, but the silence afterward.

A while later, Kick's husband, the Duke of Devonshire, will be killed by a German sniper. At twenty-five, Kick is a widow. When she finds happiness again it will be short-lasting—she and her married lover, Lord Peter Fitzwilliam, die in a plane crash over France in 1948.

Death seems to be tugging at the Kennedys' heels.

Joe Sr. and Rose didn't approve of their daughter marrying Billy Hartington, the Duke of Devonshire, because he wasn't Catholic. Joe Jr. (right) attended the wedding.

chapter **5**

A Political Career Begins

Jack steps into his brother's shoes as the oldest child, but he is still as directionless as a weathervane. Should he go to law school like Joe Jr. or become a businessman like his father? Or should he work toward fulfilling the dream that his father held for his brother Joe—to become the first Irish-Catholic president of the United States? And, frankly, with a father like Joe Kennedy, does he really have a choice?

Jack enrolls in the Stanford University graduate business school and takes courses in economics but leaves after the first semester. Then he spends time in the hospital dealing with the results of a failed operation on his back. Always a natural writer, Jack covers the establishment of the United Nations in San Francisco in 1945 for Hearst newspapers and is then assigned to cover the British elections in London, as well as the Potsdam Conference, where the Allies make decisions about how to deal with defeated Germany. Times are changing and Churchill loses the election. With F.D.R.'s death during his fourth

Harry S. Truman is sworn in as the thirty-third president of the United States of America following the death of F.D.R.

term as president, the United States, too, has a new leader in Harry Truman. Truman speeds up the end of the war by ordering the U.S. military to drop an atomic bomb on Hiroshima, Japan, on August 6, 1945. Three days later a second bomb is dropped on Nagasaki. Japan surrenders. The war is over.

In the summer of 1945, Jack decides to run for public office as a Democrat.

Two seats look like strong possibilities: lieutenant governor of Massachusetts and congressman. Jack feels that with his war and other experiences overseas, he has a better shot at the latter. Plus, he'd be running for the same seat in Congress that his grandfather, Honey Fitz, had represented.

The Atomic Bomb

In 1942, the U.S. government began to secretly develop atomic bombs in a program called the Manhattan Project. President Truman ordered the dropping of two atomic bombs on Japan hoping to end the war quickly and minimize the number of American lives lost. This was a very controversial decision. The bombs destroyed two cities, killed 115,000 people, and poisoned many more.

———————— • ————————

Jack climbs the stairs to a modest apartment in the working-class area of Charlestown, Massachusetts. Dave Powers, a war veteran, answers the door. He lives with his widowed sister and her eight children. He's on the 52-20; unemployed vets get twenty bucks per week for fifty-two weeks. Jack is looking for help in his campaign for Congress and has been told to seek out Powers, a man familiar with the 11th Congressional District. Jack takes notes when Dave talks, and a couple of days later, Dave attends Jack's talk to "gold-star" mothers, who, like Rose, have lost sons in the war. Jack and Dave take the el, and from the elevated train Dave points out the ships, the longshoremen, the stores of the working class; he gives Jack a tour of a poor neighborhood.

It doesn't take Dave long to agree to work for Jack. In fact, Powers will stay close to Jack throughout his career. Powers and other friends—Lem Billings, Torbert MacDonald, Ted Reardon, and Paul "Red" Fay—join in the campaign. Jack's sisters also help—Eunice, Pat, Jean—along with Rose, who will host house parties and teas that attract hundreds of women. The parties are so successful that there's a run on fancy dresses in the local shops, and when 1,500 women show up at a tea at the Hotel Commander in Cambridge, traffic comes to a halt. Joe Sr. does his bit by hiring a public relations firm and fueling the campaign with unlimited funds. Most

Jack, his grandfather, Honey Fitz (left), and his father, Joe Sr.: three generations of politicians and public servants.

importantly, brother Bobby joins the family tour of duty. He has just completed his service on the destroyer named for his brother, the *Joseph P. Kennedy, Jr.*, and is in charge of the East Cambridge section of the district.

Jack lives and works out of a hotel room and often conducts meetings in the bathroom while soaking in a hot bath to relieve his aching back.

Jack's opponents portray him as nothing more than a spoiled millionaire's son from Harvard who now calls a hotel room home. With his background, they say, how could he ever represent the working class? Jack shakes hands, talks, and shakes more hands. He runs up and down stairs, knocking on apartment doors. He introduces himself and asks for votes. He lives on burgers and shakes. Despite his critics, all his hard work pays off. Jack wins the primary, then the election. He's 29 years old, and his picture lands on the cover of the *New York Times* as well as *Time* magazine.

There's another new face in Congress that Jack will come to know. He's a Republican from California, and his name is Richard Nixon.

———————— • ————————

Jack's a congressman, but he's still so young looking that someone mistakes him for the elevator operator and asks

him to punch a floor. He's a kid at heart who plays baseball and touch football in his Georgetown neighborhood in Washington, D.C. He's six feet tall, 140 pounds, and clothes just hang off him; he's built like a flagpole.

In Congress, Jack is interested in social and economic issues such as housing, jobs, wages, and Social Security, and he always has an eye out for foreign policy. He fights for affordable housing for veterans who returned home to a housing shortage, but Republicans kill the bill.

After three terms in Congress, Jack decides that it's time to move on to bigger and better things. Congress is fine, but for a man like Jack, the ambassador's son with a keen sense of foreign affairs, the Senate holds more promise.

In 1952, history repeats itself…almost. Jack campaigns against Senator Henry Cabot Lodge, Jr., whose grandfather

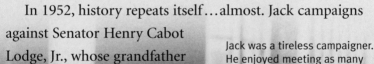

Jack was a tireless campaigner. He enjoyed meeting as many voters as possible.

SENATOR
JOHN KENNEDY

defeated Honey Fitz for the same Senate seat in 1916. Jack emphasizes foreign policy. Bobby Kennedy, who now works in the Department of Justice, agrees to manage Jack's campaign. Jack's bad back flares up and he often walks with crutches, ditching them before he walks to a podium to speak. The Kennedy women hold more successful teas—33, in fact.

> *"It was those damn tea parties that beat me."*
>
> Senator Henry Cabot Lodge, Jr.

Election night looks like a sweep by the Republicans, who ride on President Dwight D. "Ike" Eisenhower's coattails. When the polls close, Jack looks to be a loser. But by three in the morning there's a shift in the votes being counted, and by first light he's won.

Aside from politics, Jack has one other important thing on his mind—the young woman he's recently met: Jacqueline Bouvier. Jackie is beautiful, educated, from a wealthy family, and just twenty-two when they meet at a dinner party. She's also Catholic, which is a big plus and one less hurdle to get over when Jackie meets Rose. Jackie was born in Southampton, New York, educated at Miss Porter's Finishing School, Vassar College, the Sorbonne in Paris, France, and George Washington University. When Jackie was nine, her father, John Vernon Bouvier III, a wealthy stockbroker, and her mother divorced. Three years later, her mother married Hugh Auchincloss and moved to Newport, Rhode Island.

Jackie's dress, made with 50 yards of silk taffeta, was designed by African-American dressmaker Ann Lowe.

In 1947, Jackie was named debutante of the year; in fact, she out-debbed every young woman that summer and was called "Queen of the Debutantes."

In 1951, Jackie got her first job as Inquiring Camera Girl for the *Washington Times-Herald*, the same newspaper where Jack's sister Kick worked. Jack has probably never met a woman who has so many of the same characteristics as his sister. She's not like the other women Jack has dated, and Jack is no slouch when it comes to dating. In fact, he's gotten a reputation as a playboy. Women just adore him.

When Jack and Jackie marry on September 12, 1953, at St. Mary's Catholic Church in Rhode Island, it is the social event of the year. There are 800 people in the church, and 1,200 at the reception at Hammersmith Farm, the estate of Jackie's mother and stepfather. Later Rose says that it was so crowded that cars were backed up for half a mile. She thinks her new daughter-in-law is a "rather quiet and shy person and soft spoken." Bobby is the best man, and Jackie's sister, Lee, is the matron of honor. A special blessing from the pope is read.

ADDISON'S DISEASE

A hormone deficiency that results in weight loss, weakness, chronic stomach upset, and low blood pressure

When the newlyweds return to Washington, D.C., they make their home at 3321 Dent Street, a red brick three-story townhouse in Georgetown with a walled-in garden at the back where Jackie liked to garden and paint.

The wedding vow Jack and Jackie keep revisiting is "in sickness and in health." Jack is frequently ill, sometimes much more seriously than he lets on. Some years before he had been diagnosed with Addison's disease. More importantly, he has to have two back operations. He's only given a 50-50 chance of surviving the surgeries, let alone walking. During the second, Jack falls into a coma and a priest is called to give last rites. But Jack, who has been in and out of hospitals since the age of two, pulls though.

Jack recovers in Palm Springs, Florida, and the doctor teaches Jackie how to change her husband's bandages. During this time, Jack writes his second book, *Profiles in Courage*, a portrait of eight senators and the moral courage they showed when their political lives were on the line. The book, dedicated to Jackie, wins the Pulitzer Prize in 1957.

Jack signed copies of his book *Profiles in Courage*, which won a Pulitzer Prize.

"May you live in interesting times" is an ancient Chinese curse. Things couldn't have been more interesting than the political and social climate of

> **COMMUNISM**
>
> An economic system in which there is no private ownership of property or wealth and one political party controls the government

the United States in the late 1940s through the mid-1950s. At home in the U.S., civil rights issues are coming to the fore. In 1954, the Supreme Court finds school desegregation unconstitutional, and black Americans begin a struggle to change how they are treated in the eyes of the law.

Internationally, the Cold War heats up. The U.S.S.R's influence is spreading throughout Eastern Europe, and governments are changing from democracies to communist dictatorships. The struggle between the U.S.S.R. trying to influence governments to become communist while the U.S.A. tried to influence governments to become free-market democracies was called the Cold War.

Many Americans are scared that communists will somehow take over the government, and that their next-door neighbors could be sympathetic to the Soviet cause, and while "Mamie Eisenhower pink" would become the color of the day, the search for communists—reds, or pinkos, as they were also known—casts a shadow across the nation and its capital.

J. Edgar Hoover, the head of the Federal Bureau of Investigation (F.B.I.) has made the search for communists in the U.S. government an obsession. In 1950, Jack votes in favor of the McCarran Internal Security Act, which requires communist groups in the U.S. to

register with the government. Spies are found and convicted. Alger Hiss, an important democrat, is convicted of spying for the Soviet Union, as are Ethel and Julius Rosenberg, Jewish immigrants who are put to death for spying in 1953.

Jack and his father are friendly with Republican Senator Joe McCarthy. McCarthy heads up a Senate committee that holds hearings in which people are made to "name names" of members of the communist party. Many people's lives are ruined as a result of their refusal to name their friends.

But when McCarthy goes over the edge and accuses the army of shielding communists during a televised hearing, he is sunk. In June 1954, the Senate votes 67 to 22 to censure him for his methods during the hearings. The only Democrat in the Senate who doesn't vote against McCarthy—doesn't vote at all, actually— is John F. Kennedy. Some viewed this as a sign of weakness.

Senator McCarthy and his top aide, Roy Cohn, avoid being overheard during a hearing.

chapter 6

Making History in the Senate

Jack's office is in room 362 of the Old Senate Office Building in Washington, D.C., and it's always buzzing with activity. During Jack's first term he really doesn't shake things up too much, but in his second term as senator he starts to. Perhaps it's a newfound inner strength. Jack's recent brush with death may have pushed that courage forward like grass through a crack in the pavement. Maybe his popularity has something to do with it. Jack wins his second senatorial term in 1958 by an overwhelming majority; nearly three out of every four votes cast are for Kennedy.

Domestic issues are far from calm—the nation's going through a mild recession, unemployment is up, and perhaps most importantly, civil rights issues are percolating.

Bobby and Jack worked together closely throughout Jack's political career.

In the Cold War, the United States appears to be coming up short in the race with Russia to develop atomic missiles, and there is a growing us-against-the-world mentality as Americans watch as communism takes over emerging nations in Southeast Asia, Africa, and Latin America.

Jack is a man with his eye on the bigger picture, so there's one place he needs to be: on the Senate Foreign Relations Committee. In his second term, Jack earns a spot on this prestigious committee, which was first established in 1816 and has played a part in shaping America's foreign policy ever since. Jack uses it as a platform to attack Republican President Eisenhower's diplomatic and military policies.

Jack also keeps his hand in domestic issues. He's chairman of the Senate Subcommittee on Labor and helps guide a Labor Reform Bill. He also believes strongly in the family farm and initiates surplus food distribution and

food-for-peace bills, in which the U.S. donates food to emerging nations in order to show how charitable a wealthy democracy can be.

While Jack is serving in the Senate, Bobby's career is gaining steam, too. Bobby graduated from Harvard University in 1948 and did a brief stint in the U.S. Navy. In 1950, twenty-five-year-old Bobby married Ethel Skakel, a classmate of his sister Jean's. Bobby and Ethel are a perfect match; she's not quite as rich as he is, but she's just as religious. Jack is best man at his brother's wedding. It's a stifling hot June day and, not in the best of health as usual, Jack faints.

The two brothers were not close as children. Joe Jr., Jack, and Kick held their father's attention as the first crop of Kennedy kids. Bobby was a sensitive boy among a flock of sisters, and there were concerns in the family that he may grow up to be a "sissy."

Years earlier, Joe Sr. had offered each of his children $1,000 if he or she would refrain from smoking or drinking before the age of twenty-one. Of the four boys, only Bobby collected.

Bobby doesn't really make a blip on the Kennedy radar screen until he manages Jack's successful campaign for the Senate in 1952, one year after graduating from the University of Virginia's law school.

After Jack's campaign, Bobby goes to work for Senator Joe McCarthy and his notorious chief aide, Roy Cohn. After an argument with Cohn, Bobby resigns. In 1955, he becomes chief counsel (head lawyer) of the Senate Permanent

Subcommittee on Investigations, whose job is to root out government corruption, organized crime, and racketeering—using bribery and intimidation to get people to do what you want—by the labor unions. Two years later, the Rackets Committee, short for the Select Committee on Improper Activities in the Labor or Management Field, goes after the big fish: powerful union leader Jimmy Hoffa. Jack serves on the committee, so he and Bobby work together closely. Hoffa is cleared of charges, and, in 1959, Bobby resigns from the committee. He will write a book called *The Enemy Within* about his experience fighting corruption in the labor unions.

Then Bobby will have another job to tackle: running a presidential campaign.

It's 1956, and Jack is thinking about taking his political career to the next level. He is considering a run for vice

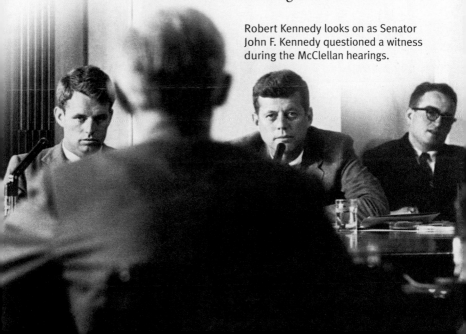

Robert Kennedy looks on as Senator John F. Kennedy questioned a witness during the McClellan hearings.

Vice Presidential Contenders in 1956
Estes Kefauver of Tennessee; Albert Gore, Sr. of Tennessee; Robert F. Wagner, Jr. of New York; Hubert Humphrey of Minnesota; and John F. Kennedy of Massachusetts.

president. At the 1956 Democratic National Convention in Chicago, Jack hopes to join Adlai Stevenson on the Democratic ticket. Who, exactly, is Adlai Stevenson?

The short answer is that this former governor of Illinois is the popular hope of Democrats for defeating the Republican ticket of President Eisenhower and Vice President Richard M. Nixon. But while Jack is destined for great things, Stevenson will enter the history books as a footnote, under the heading of "what might have been." Jack thinks being vice president will hold his attention until it's time to run for president in 1960. Joe Sr., however, has not raised a son to be content with being vice anything.

To Joe, with his keen political eye, it looks like Stevenson will get creamed by Eisenhower in the election. Plus, if Jack loses, his father doesn't want it blamed on Jack's religion. At the convention,

Jack presented Adlai Stevenson's nomination at the 1956 Democratic National Convention.

1956
DEMOCRATIC

Jack feels the power and the momentum. He's comfortable addressing crowds. He has got what every leader needs: people willing to follow. He's got the pulse and the drumbeat. Should he or shouldn't he try to get the vice-presidential nomination? Jack sends Bobby off to phone their father for advice, and Joe thinks it's the worst idea possible. Joe is furious, and you can imagine Bobby having to pull the phone away from his ear when Joe speaks his mind. But Jack sticks to his instincts and decides to go for it.

Jack polled members of the Massachusetts delegation at the convention.

Jack is endorsed by the *Chicago Sun-Times*, and momentum builds. But he loses the nomination to Senator Estes Kefauver when Stevenson allows the delegates to choose the candidate.

Jack may have lost the battle, but he's going to win the war. To millions of people watching the convention at home on their televisions, Jack comes off as a winner: humble, intelligent, witty and, perhaps…presidential.

After the convention, Jack takes off for a vacation in France without his wife. This is not the best move. Jackie, seven months pregnant, goes into labor prematurely, and the baby, a little girl, dies. This is the second child they have lost;

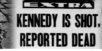

Jackie's first pregnancy ended in a miscarriage. Jackie is in critical condition, and Jack is out at sea on vacation and can't be reached. Bobby, always dependable and always there for Jackie, stays at her side until Jack returns.

Jackie feels sad and lonely in their home, a huge mansion in Virginia called Hickory Hill. A few months later, Jack and Jackie sell the home to Bobby and Ethel, who already have a handful of children. It could not have been an easy time for Jackie, who desperately wanted a family of her own.

The following year, on November 27, 1957, a perfect little girl is born to Jackie and Jack. They name her Caroline Bouvier Kennedy.

———————— • ————————

If getting to Congress is like getting to first base, and being elected to the Senate is like getting to second or third, then Jack wants to hit a home run. His father Joe and other advisers meet in Hyannis Port, Massachusetts, as well as in Palm Beach, Florida, to decide on strategy.

On January 2, 1960, Jack declares himself a candidate for the presidency. Two hurdles are familiar: his religion and his age. But he's got a third hurdle this time, a strong opponent named Hubert Humphrey.

Humphrey, senator from Minnesota, first caught national attention when he gave an impassioned pro-civil rights speech at the 1948 Democratic Convention. Humphrey is convinced he can win the Democratic primary in his neighboring state of Wisconsin. (Primaries are elections

political parties hold to help decide who their candidates will be.) Unfortunately for Humphrey, the Kennedy Express, complete with Rose and Jack's sisters, pulls into Wisconsin. The ladies will repeat their famous teas and house parties from his earlier campaigns. Jackie's here, too, and in Kenosha, she addresses supermarket shoppers over the store's public address system to tell them all about her husband and why they should vote for him. Imagine going in to buy hamburger and being treated to that!

The young Kennedy family visited Hyannis Port in November 1960.

Jack wins the primary in one of the biggest victories the state has ever seen.

Next stop: West Virginia. If Jack can win here, in a state that's almost one hundred percent Protestant, then he can probably win anywhere. At this time, some people thought a Catholic president would take orders from the pope, the leader of the Catholic church.

Jack had risked his life in the Navy in World War II, and his brother had died serving the nation; how could anybody, he asks, doubt his loyalty to the United States? Religion wasn't a factor when Joe Jr. was being strapped into the plane for his final mission. Humphrey chooses "Give Me That Old Time Religion" as his campaign theme song, to add fuel to the fire. Clearly, the gloves have come off.

Kennedy smiles from a campaign poster.

In West Virginia, Jack gets his hands dirty…literally. In a state known for its mining industry, Jack visits ghostlike mining towns and is even lowered into a mine shaft. Jack sees poverty and hopelessness firsthand.

As he's done ever since he was a child, he charms the crowds. Eleanor Roosevelt and her son, Franklin Delano Roosevelt, Jr., lend their support, and Jack wins

the West Virginia primary. Hubert Humphrey drops out of the race.

Four men arrive in Los Angeles to try to win the Democratic nomination for president—Adlai Stevenson, Lyndon Johnson, Stuart Symington, and John F. Kennedy— but only one would leave with the prize. Jack arrives aboard his private plane, the *Caroline*, and soon his supporters are handing out tie clips in the shape of *PT-109*. Jack may be the youngest of the bunch, but he is also the wittiest, brightest, and sharpest.

Conventions are noisy, crowded, and boisterous events that demonstrate democracy in action. It is here that the future is decided by open vote. This convention, from July 11 to 15, 1960, in Los Angeles, California, is a sea of confetti, of Kennedy posters raised high on wooden handles, of straw hats with red, white, and blue ribbons. There is electricity in the air.

Jack needs 761 votes to clinch the nomination. Each state gets a chance to commit its delegates' votes. When it is Wyoming's turn, that state commits all fifteen of its delegates to Jack. That puts him over the top by two votes. He wins on the first ballot, with 806 votes total. His campaign theme song, "Happy Days Are Here Again," is about to play.

Outside Looking In

Outside the arena where the convention was being held, more than 5,000 protestors, including Dr. Martin Luther King, Jr., and Bayard Rustin, the organizer of the 1963 March on Washington, demonstrated in support of civil rights and for the greater presence of such rights in the Democratic platform and party.

Texas senator Lyndon Johnson, who Jack will name as his vice-presidential running mate, will come in second, with 409 votes. Though rivals during the primary, they team up to form the Democratic presidential ticket. Jack needs Johnson to help get votes in the South.

Standing in California, the end of the frontier for the pioneers and settlers of an earlier century, Jack evokes a new frontier in his acceptance speech. His words calling for citizens to take an active role in society will come to define the Kennedy

In his speech accepting the presidential nomination, Jack told America that "We shall carry the fight to the people....And we shall win."

CRATIC NATIONAL CONV

spirit: "[The New Frontier] sums up not what I intend to offer the American people, but what I intend to ask of them....But I tell you the New Frontier is here, whether we seek it or not. Beyond that frontier are the uncharted areas of science and space, unsolved problems of peace and war, unconquered pockets of ignorance and prejudice, unanswered questions of poverty and surplus.

Jackie, who was pregnant, decided to stay home during the convention. She met the press on the evening of July 14 at the Kennedy compound in Hyannis Port.

"It would be easier to shrink back from that frontier, to look to the safe mediocrity of the past, to be lulled by good intentions and high rhetoric—and those who prefer that course should not cast their votes for me, regardless of party.

"But I believe the times demand new invention, innovation, imagination, decision. I am asking each of you to be pioneers on that New Frontier. My call is to the young in heart, regardless of age—to all who respond to the Scriptural call: 'Be strong and of a good courage; be not afraid, neither be thou dismayed.'"

chapter 7

Kennedy v. Nixon

The Democrats aren't the only ones busy picking a presidential candidate. The Republicans choose Vice President Richard M. Nixon as their man. Nixon's running mate is none other than Kennedy nemesis Henry Cabot Lodge, Jr. When they say history repeats itself, did they mean this soon?

Nixon agrees to go up against Jack in a series of four televised presidential debates, the first of which is held on September 26, 1960.

Why does Nixon accept Jack's challenge in the first place? His advisers urge him to decline since he's the incumbent and has less to prove than Jack.

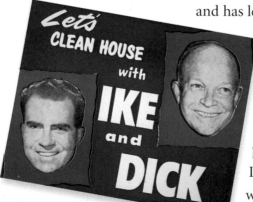

Richard "Dick" Nixon served as Eisenhower's vice president for two terms.

But Nixon thinks he knows better. He is an experienced debater. Plus, he hadn't been that impressed with Jack's performance at the Democratic Convention, where some thought Jack spoke on matters that were too complicated to be understood by your average TV viewer.

Nixon smelled blood and accepted the challenge. Besides, he had already proven himself before the television cameras; in his "Checkers Speech" of 1952, he had answered charges of improper conduct while in office, saving his political career.

Aside from party affiliation, there is another striking difference between the two men. While Jack gathered the best and the brightest men around him as advisers and took their advice, Nixon is someone who does not trust people. Jack is smart enough to know how to benefit from the smarts of other people; Nixon doesn't like to show his cards.

Seventy million people will tune in to watch Kennedy and Nixon debate in what would be the largest TV audience for a political event to date. The United States had come a long way in the more than one hundred years since the historic debates between

Nixon and Checkers

On September 23, 1952, Nixon addressed the nation to answer charges that he had used $18,000 in campaign funds for personal expenses. After making a complete account of his finances, Nixon explained that a cocker spaniel had been sent to the Nixon daughters after his wife, Pat Nixon, had talked on the radio about how her daughters wanted a dog. Nixon said that while Checkers had been a personal gift from a supporter, they refused to give him back, since the girls loved him so much.

Abraham Lincoln and Stephen A. Douglas in 1858.

Nixon arrives by car at the Chicago TV station where the first debate will take place. As he gets out of the car, he bangs his knee badly. He has

"I think the question before the American people is: Are we doing as much as we can do?"

John F. Kennedy, from the first debate

recently recovered from knee surgery, so this knock-up is not what he needs. Plus, he lost weight after the surgery, so he looks a little gaunt.

The use of television made style a part of the debate. And frankly, Nixon does not score too highly in that category. His light gray suit does not film well, and he comes off looking a bit pale, if not queasy. Jack's dark suit, by contrast, looks good on the tube, and gives him a visual advantage, an aura of strength. When Jack, trim and sporting a Hyannis Port summer tan, declines makeup before the debate, so does Nixon. Big mistake.

The amazing thing about this contest is that most people who watched it on TV thought Kennedy had won; those listening on the radio declared

Kennedy said, "I believe in 1960 and '61 and two and three we have a rendezvous with destiny."

Nixon the winner. And Rose, well, she thinks Jack came off like a young Lincoln.

Though Nixon's performance improved during the three debates that followed, people were so impressed with Jack during the first one that the others had less impact.

———————— • ————————

What are Jack's greatest obstacles to becoming president? He's young, Catholic, and unlike Richard Nixon, who is in his second term as vice president, Jack has not served in the executive branch of government.

> "What will determine whether Senator Kennedy or I, if I am elected, was a great president?" said Nixon. "It will be determined to the extent that we represent the deepest ideals, the highest feelings and faith of the American people."

With less than a month to go till the election, Kennedy-Johnson and Nixon-Lodge are neck and neck. Jack keeps his cool, but Nixon seems to have taken on the characteristics the nation saw in the debates: He is slouchy, angry, and ashen. It is as if Jack is being produced in Technicolor, while Nixon is still being shot in black-and-white.

Jack always goes the extra mile, literally. In ten months of campaigning he clocks more than 75,000 miles aboard the *Caroline*. He reaches out to as many people as possible. His lead slips a bit when President Eisenhower offers Nixon last-minute support. So Jack shakes more hands,

> ## *"Give me your voice, your hand, your vote."*
>
> From Kennedy's 1960 campaign brochure

gives more speeches, and gets less sleep.

What kind of world would the next president inherit from the Republican team of Eisenhower-Nixon? First, the economy had been in a coma since the mid to late 1950s. Unemployment was on the rise. The buzzing postwar economy was over.

In the South, African-Americans regularly held demonstrations demanding civil rights. The mostly peaceful protest often turned violent when racist mobs and sometimes police attacked the protestors.

Around the world it was tense, too. In May 1960, the Soviet military had shot down an American spy plane and captured pilot Gary Powers; an emergency summit then collapsed between Eisenhower and Soviet Premier Nikita Khrushchev; in Cuba, only ninety miles away from the Florida coast, Dictator Fidel Castro, with the help of the Soviet Union, is becoming a threat to the United States. It seems like the strongest nation to emerge from the Cold War may be the one who can flex the biggest nuclear arms.

SUMMIT

A summit is a conference between high-level officials where problems are talked out in an effort to solve them or come to an agreement.

Clearly, the time for Jack's New Frontier is now.

On November 8, 1960—Election Day—Jack and Jackie

cast their votes at a branch of the Boston public library, then head back to Hyannis Port to watch the results. Bobby's house is set up as command central for the press, with more than two dozen phones and a handful of Teletype machines. As the night wears on, it's a toss-up between Kennedy and Nixon. First the good news: Jack takes Connecticut by at least 100,000 votes. The bad news: He's slipping in the Midwest and the farm belt. It's nail-biting time for everyone, except for Jack, who keeps his cool and smokes a good Havana cigar.

Jack goes to bed in the early hours of the morning when the election is still too close to call.

John F. Kennedy accepted the nomination for president before an enthusiastic crowd of Democratic supporters.

"For of those to whom much is given, much is required."

There are a few undecided states, including California, Nixon's home turf, plus Illinois, Minnesota, and Michigan. Nixon takes California, but victories in the other three states give Jack the electoral votes he needs.

At 4:30 AM, Secret Service agents arrive to protect the president-elect. Jack is the youngest man and the first Catholic to be elected president of the United States. In the morning, Caroline greets her dad as "Mr. President."

The election is a victory for Jack, but it isn't the landslide he may have hoped for. He defeats Nixon by only a slim margin where the total number of votes counted came close to 69 million.

At the end of the month, the Kennedys have more good news. On November 25, John Jr., called "John John," is born, and shortly afterward the soon-to-be first family takes off for Palm Beach. There, Jackie can recover and Jack can plan for the new administration.

Nixon and Kennedy were cool customers during the race for president. The 1960 election featured new and novel political ads.

On the night of January 19, 1961, a huge storm hits Washington, D.C. It's the night before the inauguration, and the city is blanketed in snow.

The morning of the inaugural, the snow has stopped, but it is bitterly cold. Jack is still working on his speech. The Kennedys leave their home in Georgetown to meet the Eisenhowers at the White House.

On election night 1960, CBS anchorman Walter Cronkite conferred with Grant Holcomb in front of a giant board showing the state-by-state voting.

On the steps of the U.S. Capitol, the inaugural ceremonies begin with a prayer from Cardinal Cushing, the singing of the national anthem by African-American contralto Marian Anderson, and the reading of "Dedication" by 89-year-old poet Robert Frost. But because of the stinging wind and bright sun, Frost cannot read the poem he wrote for the occasion; instead he recites his patriotic poem "The Gift Outright" from memory.

Shortly after noon, Chief Justice Earl Warren administers the oath of office, and John F. Kennedy

Voting in the 1960 Presidential Election

John F. Kennedy: 34,226,731 popular votes (49.9%)

Richard M. Nixon: 34,108,157 popular votes (49.7%)

is sworn in as president of the United States. Jack stands coatless and hatless and the word *vigor* (or "vigah," as Jack pronounces it in his New England accent) defines the man, the moment, and his administration.

In preparation for the inauguration, Jack had sent two Secret Service men to Boston to retrieve the Fitzgerald family Bible. With his family by his side, with his vice president by his side, and with the old administration by his side, he addresses the nation. The New Frontier has arrived, if only we have the power to see it, he says. Jack's speech is a call to action: The 1950s are over. It's time for the new

"If more politicians knew poetry and more poets knew politics, I am convinced that the world would be a little better place to live."

John F. Kennedy

President Kennedy delivered his inaugural speech before a crowd of 50,000 people.

generation to participate in the future. Toward the end of his 14-minute address, Jack speaks the words that will become part of his legacy:

"And so, my fellow Americans: Ask not what your country can do for you—ask what you can do for your country.

"My fellow citizens of the world: Ask not what America will do for you, but what together we can do for the freedom of man."

The stakes are big. The message is clear.

A replica of *PT-109* and some of the surviving crew members had a starring role in the inaugural parade.

Had you stood on Pennsylvania Avenue on January 20, 1961, that cold and bright day, you would have stood a fair chance of seeing the new president and the first lady drive by. If you could have stood the cold, bundled up for the three-and-a-half–hour procession, you also would have seen marching bands and military parades and then, suddenly, coming down the avenue, a giant float— a replica of *PT-109* on wheels.

That night, the Kennedys attend the inaugural balls. The city is dressed in white snow, and Jack and Jackie are dressed to the nines. The festivities go on until the early morning hours.

chapter **8**

Early Days in the White House

Jack gets to work the day after the inauguration, even though it's the weekend. His campaign and election have had him in constant motion, showing what the new, younger generation can do. He puts his "vigah" to the test.

In March, Jack signs Executive Order 10925, establishing the President's Committee on Equal Employment Opportunity. The order prohibits discrimination in the hiring of federal workers and denies federal contracts to businesses that discriminate. Jack asks his vice president to chair the committee, believing Lyndon Johnson is the right person to bridge the old ways with the New Frontier. Jack can't get everything he wants passed in Congress because

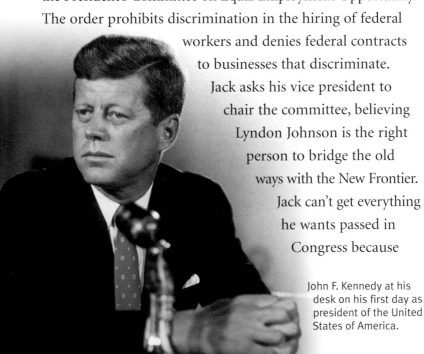

John F. Kennedy at his desk on his first day as president of the United States of America.

Congress is a mixture of Republicans and conservative Southern Democrats, neither of whom put social change at the top of the agenda. As a result, Jack's unable to do anything at the moment about education reform

Jack addressed a joint session of Congress on May 25, 1961, where he spoke of the "extraordinary challenge" facing the nation.

and health insurance for the elderly. However, he is able to help the everyday worker in America with increases to Social Security, the minimum wage, and unemployment benefits. He also gets legislation passed to help farmers, paves the way

President Kennedy's Team

The key members of JFK's senior staff and cabinet are: **Secretary of Defense** Robert McNamara; **National Security Advisor** McGeorge Bundy; **Secretary of State** Dean Rusk; **Under-secretary of State** Chester Bowles; **Attorney General** Robert F. Kennedy; **Secretary of Agriculture** Orville Freeman; **Ambassador to the U.N.** Adlai Stevenson; **Press Secretary** Pierre Salinger.

for the continued building of a national highway system, and makes a move to help the environment with a water pollution control act and the creation of the National Seashore Parks. He continues to support the Food for Peace Program to help impoverished peoples

overseas. In keeping with his belief that exercise is important, Jack founds the President's Council on Physical Fitness.

On April 10, Jack makes time to throw out the first pitch for the Washington Senators baseball team. Jack jokes that adviser Dave Powers is the "undersecretary of baseball."

Jack spends a good deal of his time in the Oval Office, located in the West Wing of the White House. Thirty feet long and twenty-five feet wide, the Oval Office has tall French windows that look out onto the Rose Garden. Sitting in a rocking chair helps Jack's aching back, so there's one here. And when he needs a workout, he visits the White House pool, which is kept to a steamy 90 degrees to help soothe his troubled back.

—————————— • ——————————

The Peace Corps stands out as one of Jack's most significant acts as president. Jack's White House is a place of ideas, and he wants those ideas spread across the globe.

Jack met with former First Lady Eleanor Roosevelt, a key figure in developing the Peace Corps.

The goal of the Peace Corps is to send energetic young Americans to foreign countries where they will roll up their sleeves and get to work teaching, building roads and bridges, and bringing their skills to the developing world. While helping others, these young people would also be acting as unofficial ambassadors, showing that America is capable of producing unselfish men and women. It would be a way of winning struggling countries to our side during the Cold War. As Jack says in an address to the nation, Peace Corps assignments will be far from easy, but they will be priceless in what young people can give and get back. The Peace Corps is established as a pilot program by an executive order on March 1, 1961. Six months later, Congress passes the law to start the program; Jack's brother-in-law, Sargent Shriver, is its first director.

The first group to go has about 500 volunteers. Less than two years later, there will be more than 5,000 volunteers working in 50 countries around the world. More than 40 years after the president's address, the Peace Corps is still making a difference.

———————— • ————————

Although at first it was believed that her expensive European tastes might turn off some voters, Jackie Kennedy becomes a beloved national icon. At home, Jackie is more fond of privacy than Jack and does not like photographers snapping pictures of John and Caroline when they're playing outside; she has tall trees planted to block even the long-distance lenses.

One of the great things about this White House is that there are two children running around and bringing life to the stodgy landmark. Caroline is known to walk into the Oval Office in her mother's high-heel shoes while Jack is conducting important business. John likes to play a game with his father where he hides in a compartment in the big desk and then pops out. Caroline has a pony on the White House grounds named Macaroni.

There's even a preschool on site where John and Caroline play and learn with other children whose parents are part of the New Frontier. The mothers take turns helping out—even Jackie, who often wears a fuzzy pink sweater all the children like to touch. Jack is a devoted father who loves to be with his children and invents stories and games for them.

Because of Jackie's love of fine art, music, and ballet, the arts come to life in the Kennedy household. They host such important musicians as Pablo Casals, Igor Stravinsky, and Isaac Stern. Artists, poets, scholars, and scientists are also invited. Ballet companies, opera

Jack and Jackie greet virtuoso violinist Isaac Stern at a White House state dinner.

divas, the Vienna Boys' Choir, and theater companies perform in the East Room. And to greet them all: Jack wears white tie and tails and Jackie looks beautiful in chic gowns.

When a high school student asks Jack if he has an "in" at a popular magazine that keeps putting his family on the cover, Jack says no, he just has a beautiful wife.

The First Lady Derby?

Jackie was sometimes uncomfortable in the role of first lady. As the story goes, she thought the term *first lady* sounded like the name of a horse! Jackie was wealthy and well educated, and some of Jack's advisers worried she would have trouble connecting with voters. However, Jackie was such a kind person that Americans loved her charm and admired her talents.

Jackie undertakes a big project to restore the interior of the White House, and a camera crew from CBS comes to film the first lady giving a tour of the results. The tour is broadcast in February 1962, and America is enthralled by Jackie and the project she holds close to her heart. As she says, it is a reverence for both beauty and history that drives her.

When the Kennedys moved in, the White House was not in the best of shape; plaster was cracking, rooms were in disarray, and the furniture was shabby.

Jackie sets up a fine arts commission and solicits donations of historic, period furniture from sources around the world. Jackie rummages through storage in the White

85

KENNEDY IS SHOT, REPORTED DEAD

"It would be a sacrilege merely to 'redecorate' the White House. It must be restored—and that has nothing to do with decoration. That is a question of scholarship."

Jacqueline Kennedy

House basement for important items. From these underground searches, she retrieves the desk that Jack will use in the Oval Office—the one that John John likes to hide in.

When the restoration is finished, Jackie, in a beautiful red dress, leads TV viewers through the Diplomatic Reception Room, the East Room, the red, white, blue, and gold corridor to the State Dining Room, through the Red Room and the Blue Room, and to perhaps the most famous room of all, the Lincoln Bedroom, a favorite of presidents and their guests.

Fifty million people tune in to see the program, and in the days and weeks following, more than 10,000 children write Jackie letters about it. And Jackie—with a little help from her staff—writes back.

There is, however, a part of America that seems to be left behind the New Frontier. Beginning with the Supreme Court's 1954 decision in *Brown v. Board of Education* of Topeka, Kansas, which declared segregation in the public schools unconstitutional, civil rights and the struggles of African-Americans become central issues in American society. African-American men fought in the trenches of Europe and the Pacific in World War II, but back home in the heavily segregated South, they could not drink from the same water fountains as whites, and they were forced to ride at the back of public buses. Rosa Parks's arrest in 1955 for refusing to give her seat to a white man led to the Montgomery bus boycotts. Martin Luther King, Jr., president of the Southern Christian Leadership Conference, organized the boycott, calling for peaceful protests.

On October 19, 1960, before Jack is elected president, Dr. Martin Luther King, Jr., is sentenced to four months of hard labor in jail for a minor traffic violation. He is led off to prison in chains. His distraught wife, five months pregnant, calls a member of the Kennedy campaign.

The TV special was shot in black-and-white, so the audience didn't know Jackie's dress was bright red.

Jack offers his support to Mrs. King. Secretly, Bobby Kennedy calls the judge and asks for King's release. Dr. King is let out the next

morning, and his father, an influential Baptist preacher who goes by the name of Daddy King, throws his support to candidate Kennedy. The votes of African-Americans prove to be a major boost to Jack on election night in 1960.

In May of 1961, the Freedom Riders of CORE, the Congress of Racial Equality, set out by Greyhound bus from Washington, D.C., to protest continued segregation on buses. They are arrested, beaten, and one bus is even bombed. Bobby Kennedy, who as attorney general heads up the Justice Department, sends an assistant, John Seigenthaler,

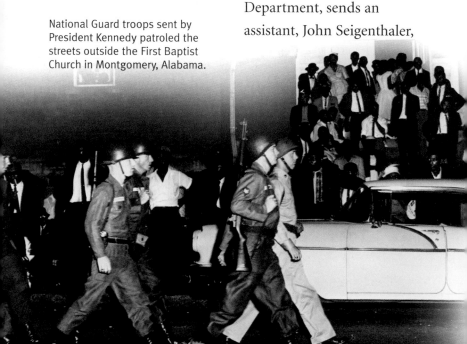

National Guard troops sent by President Kennedy patroled the streets outside the First Baptist Church in Montgomery, Alabama.

to keep on eye on the protests. Seigenthaler is beaten into a coma by angry, racist mobs at the Montgomery, Alabama, bus station. Following all the violence, Dr. King is expected to speak at the First Baptist Church. The Freedom Riders and their supporters are surrounded by angry mobs who trap them in the church. Jack and Bobby send in National Guard troops to protect them.

Martin Luther King, Jr.

Dr. Martin Luther King, Jr., was a minister and civil rights leader. In the 1963 March on Washington, King led more than 250,000 people to Washington, D.C., to demand equal rights for African-Americans. It was here that Dr. King stirred the nation with his "I Have a Dream" speech. He fought for civil rights until he was assassinated in 1968.

Scenes like these would happen many times over the next years while brave Americans worked to integrate the South.

On June 11, 1963, Jack addresses the nation, asking for support in his quest to have Congress pass legislation that permanently integrates public facilities in America. "The heart of the question is whether all Americans are to be afforded equal rights and equal opportunities, whether we are going to treat our fellow Americans as we want to be treated. If an American, because his skin is dark, cannot eat lunch in a restaurant open to the

> *"This nation will move forward, with the full speed of freedom, in the exciting adventure of space."*
>
> John F. Kennedy, May 25, 1961

public, if he cannot send his children to the best public school available, if he cannot vote for the public officials who will represent him, if, in short, he cannot enjoy the full and free life which all of us want, then who among us would be content to have the color of his skin changed and stand in his place? Who among us would then be content with the counsels of patience and delay?"

———————— • ————————

Apparently, the New Frontier extends thousands of miles into space. Jack has dreams of putting a man on the moon before the 1960s end. At this point the Russians are leading the space race. Soviet satellite Sputnik I orbited the earth in 1957, and four years later Soviet cosmonaut Yuri Gagarin was the first man to circle the earth.

America's first astronauts: Shepard is at back left, and Glenn is in the front row, third from left.

The race to the moon is on. Jack wants America not only to catch up to the Russians' progress, he wants to pass them. His top priority is that America have a lunar landing before the Soviets do.

In fact, in a conversation with James Webb, the head of the National Air and Space Administration during the Kennedy years, Jack makes it clear that beating the Soviets to the moon isn't *a* priority, it's *the* priority.

On May 25, 1961, Jack addresses a joint session of Congress: "First, I believe that this nation should commit itself to achieving the goal, before this decade is out, of landing a man on the moon and returning him safely to the earth. No single space project in this period will be more impressive to mankind, or more important for the long-range exploration of space; and none will be so difficult or expensive to accomplish."

That year, Alan Shepard, the astronaut who made the first manned space flight for the United States, receives the NASA Distinguished Service Medal from Jack in a White House ceremony.

On February 20, 1962, John Glenn becomes the first American to orbit the earth. Back home, Glenn also receives the Distinguished Service Medal and is treated to a hero's welcome with a ticker-tape parade in New York City.

A Mercury Atlas rocket at Cape Canaveral, Florida

chapter **9**

J.F.K. and the World

The first international challenge to the new administration comes early and is an inheritance from Eisenhower's days in office. More than 1,000 Cuban exiles, who had left Cuba because they disagreed with communist dictator Fidel Castro, have been trained by the Central Intelligence Agency (CIA) under director Richard Bissell. Their goal is to invade Cuba at the Bay of Pigs and overthrow Castro. The plan fails, and 114 of the exiles die in the invasion; 1,189 are captured and jailed. Jack takes full responsibility for the operation because he gave it the green light. Despite having reservations, he had listened to advisers who urged him to go forward with the plan. It was a mistake for Jack not to trust his instincts.

He is concerned about how the world will view this failure by a new, young president. His thoughts turn to Soviet leader Nikita Khrushchev, who plays

Cuba exiles demonstrated outside a hotel where Kennedy was staying to win help for their cause—getting Castro out of power and eliminating communism in Cuba.

the role of puppetmaster to Castro's puppet.

Why would a little island take so much of the focus of the Kennedy administration? The main reason is that the Soviets had a lot of influence on Castro and the Soviet Union had become the U.S.'s main

The Cuban exiles who survived the failed Bay of Pigs operation led by the U.S., were captured and held as prisoners of war by Castro.

rival for world power during the Cold War. Plus, Cuba was so close to the United States—only 90 miles off the coast of Florida—that it posed a greater threat than communist nations in Europe and Asia.

Who Is Fidel Castro?

Fidel Castro Ruz was born on August 13, 1926 or 1927 (sources disagree), and studied at Jesuit schools as a boy. He later earned a law degree from the University of Havana and married into one of Cuba's wealthiest families. In the early 1950s, Castro opposed the military dictatorship of General Fulgencio Batista by peaceful means, but when this did not succeed, he led a revolution that brought down Batista in 1958. Castro rose to power and began to take over American-owned property in Cuba, leading the U.S. to break off relations. Castro turned to Soviet premier Khrushchev for help, paving the way for a showdown with the U.S.

Khrushchev and Kennedy met in Vienna on June 4, 1961, to hammer out agreements on nuclear weapons and other issues.

The Kennedys and their advisers want Castro out of office, if not dead. There are tales of poison cigars and other secret plans to get rid of Castro. In a 1975 congressional investigation known as the Church committee, more than six plots to kill Castro came to light. Forty years later, Castro is still in power.

It's spring of 1961, and Jack is going on a trip to Europe to meet Soviet Premier Nikita Khrushchev in Vienna. On his way, Jack stops in Paris to meet with French president Charles de Gaulle. De Gaulle, a hero of World War II, would like France to develop nuclear weapons. Jack does not think that's a good idea. They talk about other things, too, such as making the French colony of Algiers independent.

At Jack's side is his secret weapon—not a suitcase with atomic codes or top-secret notes. Jack's got Jackie by his side, and she is about to take Paris by storm. Because of her French ancestry, fluent spoken French, and her grace and style, the French line up by the thousands to catch a glimpse of her. She stuns them with her beauty at a state dinner at Versailles, a grand museum that was once the home of France's kings

and queens. It's neck and neck as to who the more popular Kennedy is. Jack will joke that history will remember him as the man who accompanied Jacqueline Kennedy to Paris.

The Kennedys head to Vienna for the summit with the Soviets. Jack has at least two problems going into the meeting. First, he's a lot younger than Khrushchev and has less experience in politics. Second, Jack bungled the Bay of Pigs invasion, and Khrushchev knows it.

At the meeting, the leaders plan to talk about ending nuclear weapons testing and forming a strategy for Berlin. After World War II, the German city of Berlin was placed under the control of Allied forces: the United States, the Soviet Union, England, and France. The Soviets were put in charge of East Berlin, while the others controlled West Berlin. Khrushchev now wants all foreign troops to leave except the Soviets. This would mean that millions of West Berliners would be forced to live under a communist system of government; Jack will never agree. During their talk Jack notices medals pinned to Khrushchev's jacket and asks what they are. When Khrushchev replies that they are peace prizes, Jack tells him that he hopes he gets to keep them, and the men laugh.

The laughter doesn't last long. The meetings don't go well, and J.F.K. thinks they have a cold winter ahead of them.

A year and a half after the European tour, Jack gets another chance to confront Castro—and Khrushchev.

On Tuesday, October 16, 1962, Jack, still in his bathrobe eating breakfast, gets word from George McBundy, the national

EXTRA
KENNEDY IS SHOT,
REPORTED DEAD

ExComm members spent hours on end meeting in the Cabinet Room in the White House during the crisis.

security advisor, that the United States has photographs of Soviet missile sites in Cuba. The pictures show enough missile power to kill more than 80 million Americans in the space of a few minutes. The clock is ticking.

At first the Soviets deny the missiles are there at all, and then they say they are there to defend Cuba from attack. Jack, with evidence from U-2 spy planes, thinks differently. He forms an advisory team of 21 senior government officials known as the Executive Committee of the National Security Council, or ExComm, for short. This group includes Vice President Johnson, U.N. Ambassador Stevenson, and Attorney General Robert Kennedy.

By Thursday, the situation looks worse, and ExComm is considering a military strike on Cuba. But first, a plan is suggested to blockade Soviet ships, and the U.S. Navy deploys 180 of its own ships

"...but the greatest danger of all would be to do nothing."

John F. Kennedy, in response to concerns about challenging the Soviets

to stop and search all ships approaching Cuba. Jack wants to do anything to avoid a nuclear war.

Though Washington would be the first target of a Soviet nuclear bomb, Jackie makes the decision to stay with Jack.

Jack addresses the nation on TV and lets the country know how serious the situation is. In the speech, he demands that

MEDIUM RANGE BALLISTIC MISSILE BASE IN CUBA
SAN CRISTOBAL

LAUNCH POSITION

MISSILE-READY TENTS

MISSILE ERECTORS

LATE OCTOBER

Top: A U.S. spy plane photographed missile sites at San Cristobal, Cuba.
Left: A news map showed the range of missiles if launched from Cuba toward the U.S.

Khrushchev remove the missiles from Cuba.

On October 24, Soviet ships approach Cuba. Most turn away because of the blockade, but some continue on. A message arrives from Khrushchev. He will agree to Jack's demands to remove the missiles, if the U.S. agrees not to invade Cuba. Jack agrees.

After holding its breath for almost two weeks, the world lets out a sigh of relief. A disaster has been avoided. In Khrushchev's eyes, Jack is now a real world leader.

In June 1963, Jack goes to Germany to talk about democracy in this divided land where the communists rule one half of Berlin and there is democracy in the other half.

Since World War II, more than three million people have fled East Berlin for West Berlin. In 1961, Khrushchev erects a huge concrete wall

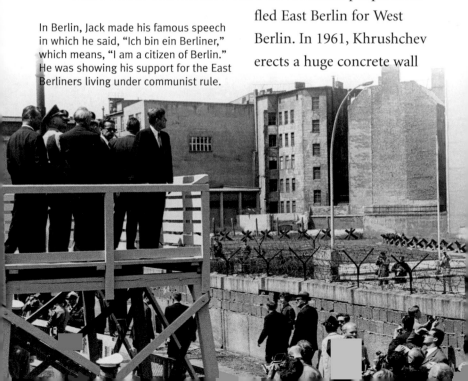

In Berlin, Jack made his famous speech in which he said, "Ich bin ein Berliner," which means, "I am a citizen of Berlin." He was showing his support for the East Berliners living under communist rule.

topped with barbed wire through the city to stop the flow of freedom seekers.

When Jack goes to West Berlin the crowds are wild for him. More than 1.5 million people line the streets to hear him speak. They shout "Ken-ne-dy! Ken-ne-dy!" Although

An index card with Kennedy's notes for the Berlin speech. A German journalist helped him translate "Ich bin ein Berliner."

democracy has its flaws, Jack says to the crowds, "We have never had to put up a wall to keep our people in!"

Other challenges from around the globe hit the administration. Will Laos, in Southeast Asia, in the midst of civil war, fall to the communists? South Vietnam, a political hot spot since the 1950s, also occupies Jack's time. The communist government in North Vietnam is threatening to invade the pro-democracy South. In 1961, Jack sends Vice President Johnson and U.S. military advisers to check out the situation, which increasingly seems to favor the communists.

And the arms race that has always symbolized the Cold War is back in the news. Jack wants a nuclear test-ban treaty with the Soviets. In July 1963, the U.S., U.S.S.R., and Great Britain, agree in principle to ban atmospheric testing of nuclear weapons. At the end of the month, the three nations sign a treaty in Moscow—one moment of progress in difficult times.

chapter **10**

"The President Has Been Shot!"

Jack needs to go to Texas because next year, 1964, is an election year, and he wants to make a nice gesture to the Democratic Party. Here are some of the words he wrote for the trip: "The historic bonds which link Texas and the Democratic Party are no temporary union of convenience," he writes. "They are deeply embedded in the history and purpose of this state and party."

The Kennedys and the Connallys (Governor Connally is in foreground) settled into the convertible limo at the airport. Then the motorcade headed to downtown Dallas.

Jack won Texas in 1960 only because he wisely chose a southern running mate, Texan Lyndon Johnson. A few weeks before Jack arrives in Texas, Adlai Stevenson, ambassador to the U.N., visits Texas and is greeted by angry crowds who are hostile to the Kennedy administration. One man manages to strike Stevenson on the head. Stevenson advises Jack to skip the Texas trip, as does the Secret Service, who have learned of death threats against the president. Some people have bad feelings toward Jack because of his role in the civil rights movement. Security is tightened.

Despite all this, Jack decides that it's necessary for him to go and bring Jackie along. It will be the first time Jack and Jackie take a trip together since the death of their son Patrick—who died two days after his birth—three months earlier.

On November 21, they land in San Antonio, where Jackie speaks to the waiting crowd in Spanish. In Fort Worth some people carry signs that read BAN THE BROTHERS and KENNEDY, KHRUSHCHEV, AND KING.

On their second day in Texas, Air Force One, the presidential plane, lands at Love Field, right outside of Dallas. Jackie wears a pink suit with a pink hat and people lining the streets call her name. She turns her head, she waves, she tries to make contact with as many people as possible. At least 250,000 people come out to see the president and first lady.

In the front seat of the convertible car they are riding in, Governor John Connally and his wife, Nellie, also wave to the crowd. The day is warmer than expected, and Jack decides to

forgo the bulletproof protective bubble, so he can easily see and be seen. Secret Service men ride all around.

The motorcade heads from Houston Street onto Elm, toward a grassy area called Dealey Plaza. Jack's got a 12:30 PM appointment at the Dallas Trade Mart, where he is scheduled to deliver a speech. Mrs. Connally turns to the president in the backseat and says, "Mr. President, you certainly cannot say that Dallas doesn't love you."

Then come the gunshots that change everything. A bullet hits Jack in the back of the neck. Connally, in the front seat, is hit in the back, then the wrist, then in the leg. Another bullet strikes Jack in the back of his head, and he slumps to the side. The back brace Jack wears keeps him upright in the seat, making him a target for the last, devastating bullet. Had he been able to flop forward, that bullet may have missed his skull.

Jackie, crying, "Oh, no," tries to cradle her husband's head and then flees to the trunk of the car. She is pushed back into the car by Secret Service agent Clint Hill, who climbs into the car and shields the president's body. Jack's car speeds to

Presidential Assassination

Presidents have long been targets for assassination. Ever since the attempted murder of Andrew Jackson, the seventh president of the United States, in 1835, four presidents have been assassinated and six others have been wounded.

Apparently, Abraham Lincoln received more than 10,000 death threats during his years in office. He kept them in an envelope marked ASSASSINATIONS.

Parkland Hospital, but Jack doesn't really stand a chance. Jackie's suit is soaked with blood.

Officially, Jack is pronounced dead at one PM, about twenty minutes after he arrives at the hospital. John Connally is seriously wounded but will live. When veteran CBS television anchor Walter Cronkite

Lyndon Johnson was sworn in on board Air Force One. New First Lady Lady Bird Johnson (left) and Jackie looked on.

announces the death of the president, he is shaken to tears.

Later, Jackie is back at Love Field where Air Force One is waiting to take her back to Washington, D.C. Jack's coffin is on the plane. A little after 2:30 PM, with Jackie at his side, Lyndon Johnson is sworn in as the thirty-sixth president of the United States. Jackie refuses to change her bloodstained suit; she wants to show the world what was done to her husband. She is in a state of shock.

When Air Force One lands back in Washington, Bobby is there to meet Jackie. He won't leave her side for days. When he heard the news of his brother's death, he had cried, "Why, God, why?"

⸱

Who killed President Kennedy? About a month before the president arrives in Texas, Lee Harvey Oswald gets a job as a

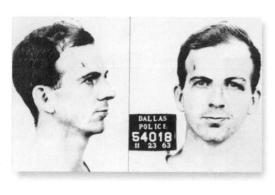

The Dallas Police Department's mug shot of Lee Harvey Oswald was taken on November 23.

clerk at the Texas School Book Depository, a dull-looking six-story building in view of Dealey Plaza. The morning of November 22, Oswald arrives at work with a long paper package. He claims he is carrying curtain rods. After the murder, he is seen running through the book depository, but since he works there, not too

A view of the Texas School Book Depository from the location on the street where President Kennedy was assassinated.

many questions are asked. When he leaves work, though, his absence creates a stir, and police broadcast his description over their radios. Oswald kills the first police officer who confronts him, J.D. Tippit, then hides out in the Texas Theater in the Oak Bluff section of Dallas, where he is discovered and arrested. As he is dragged out of the theater, he says, "Everybody will know who I am now." The following day Oswald is charged with murdering

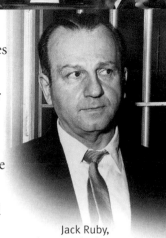

Jack Ruby, photographed a month after his arrest for killing Lee Harvey Oswald

John F. Kennedy by shooting him from the sixth floor of the Texas School Book Depository.

Oswald, a former Marine, is a believer in communism. When Jack was dealing with Cuba, Oswald was handing out leaflets that said HANDS OFF CUBA. He became so interested in the idea of communism that years before, he had moved from the United States to the Soviet Union and become a member of the Communist Party. He had married a Russian woman, Marina Prusakova, and together they moved to Texas, where their daughter was born.

Two days after Oswald kills Jack, Oswald himself is

Buzz Words

Some of the phrases used to describe J.F.K.'s assassination have become part of our everyday language. Did Lee Harvey Oswald act alone—was he "the lone gunman"? Did shots come from the "grassy knoll," an area to the right rear of the limousine? And was one of the shots a "magic bullet" because it struck Kennedy and then also Governor Connally? These terms are part of a special dialect that describes aspects of this emotional event.

shot and killed by Jack Ruby, a nightclub owner, in the basement of the city jail while being moved to the county jail. The events were captured on TV. The country, if not the world, has been glued to the TV for three days now.

"You killed my president, you rat!" Ruby shouts as he pulls the trigger. A wounded Oswald is taken to Parkland Hospital, the same hospital Jack was taken to, and dies. Ruby is found guilty of murder on November 26, and is convicted and sent to prison the following March.

John F. Kennedy's assassination is a symbol of humanity's darkest hour. How would Jack have

Jack's coffin was carried through the streets of Washington, D.C. Jackie asked aides to find out all they could about Lincoln's funeral. Many details from the 1865 event were replicated to honor Jack.

wanted to be remembered in the days, weeks, years to come?

"I am certain," Jack once said, "that after the dust of centuries has passed over our cities, we, too, will be remembered not for victories or defeats in battle or in politics, but for our contribution to the human spirit."

In the most poignant moment of the days of public mourning, John John saluted his father as the casket was carried from St. Matthew's Cathedral.

On November 24, President Kennedy's body lies in state in the Capitol Rotunda. Covered with the American flag, the coffin rests on the same bier, or platform, that held the body of Abraham Lincoln nearly one hundred years before, in 1865.

Thousands of people came to pay their respects to their slain president. Jackie and Caroline pray, then kneel at Jack's coffin. Jackie kisses the flag, while Caroline reaches her hand up to touch it.

The next day, Monday, November 25, is the funeral. Outside the White House a procession of family, statesmen, world leaders, and friends gather to walk to St. Matthew's Cathedral for mass, while Jack's casket is carried on a horse-

Anonymous notes were among the many tips the Dallas Police and other law enforcement agencies received regarding the assassination of the president.

drawn carriage. Among the dignitaries are President Charles de Gaulle of France, Queen Frederika of Greece, King Baudouin of Belgium, Emperor Haile Selassie of Ethiopia, and Prince Philip of Britain.

After the church service, Jackie leaves St. Matthew's with her children in their bright blue winter coats. The burial will take place at Arlington National Cemetery. On the steps of the cathedral, John Jr. salutes his father's coffin as it passes by. That moment becomes one of the most powerful images of the twentieth century.

For the fallen leader there is a caisson, a two-wheeled vehicle often used to haul ammunition, pulled by six gray horses. Next to this, there is a riderless black horse named Blackjack. A sword dangles by the horse's side, and its stirrups hang backward. Jackie walks with Bobby and Teddy to the cemetery, where the "Star Spangled Banner" is played by a military band. Fifty jet fighter planes tear across the sky, taps are played, and a twenty-one gun salute rings through

the air. Jackie takes a burning candle and lights the eternal flame at Jack's grave. The flame still burns today.

Behind her black veil, Jackie is a pillar of strength, showing the world that she, too, is made up of the same courage as her husband. At the end of the ceremony, the flag that covers Jack's casket is folded and given to her.

Back at the White House, she will receive the dignitaries. Also, it is her son's third birthday; there will be a small party for him.

In the hours that followed Jack's assassination, the nation turned eerily quiet. Schools let out early, businesses closed down for the day, and the feeling of shock gave over to feelings of emptiness, which gave way to anger.

———————— • ————————

Why kill Jack? Because he was Catholic and there was still so much prejudice at the time? Or perhaps because he was in favor of civil rights and wanted the New Frontier to be a place for everyone, black and white? He wanted developing nations to choose democracy over communism. Was one of these reasons reason enough to kill?

A conspiracy is a secret plot carried out by more than one person, or conspirator. Many people believe that Lee Harvey Oswald did not act alone and was part of a larger plan. With Oswald murdered, the best source of information about what had happened was gone. Enter "J.F.K. conspiracy" into a search engine and you'll get more than 150,000 returns.

Was there a man in the crowd in Dallas signaling to Oswald by opening and closing an umbrella? If so, was there more than one shooter? Was Oswald the fall guy for somebody else? Did doctors foul up at the hospital? And what about the autopsy? Why did the autopsy photographs disappear? And let's not forget about the C.I.A., or maybe even Fidel Castro, the Soviet Union, or organized crime. One theory even has Lyndon Johnson—the man who would gain the most from Jack's death—as the villain.

New president Johnson sets up the Warren Commission (officially, the President's Commission on the Assassination of President Kennedy; Executive Order 11130) one week after the assassination. Under Supreme Court Chief Justice Earl Warren, who served as chairman, the commission's job is to determine if Lee Harvey Oswald acted alone, or if there were others involved in the crime. After interviewing hundreds of witnesses and countless others, including Lyndon and Lady Bird Johnson, the commission delivers its findings on September 24, 1964. According to the Warren Commission, Lee Harvey Oswald acted alone, firing three shots from the sixth floor of the Texas School Book Depository. The first bullet misses, but the second bullet enters Jack's body at his neck, then exits and tears through Governor Connally, finally lodging in his thigh. The third bullet destroys Jack's skull.

A home movie taken by a man in the crowd, Abraham Zapruder, shows Kennedy as he was shot. The evidence of the film is used by the Warren Commission to back up its claims about the shots being fired from one source,

the book depository. But some people swore a bullet was fired from the direction of a grassy knoll nearby, which is inconsistent with the commission's findings.

There are so many unanswered questions that dozens of conspiracy theories continue to emerge, even today.

But politics, just like Monday turns into Tuesday and spring yields to summer, goes on. A year later it's time to choose the new Democratic nominee for president. Had Jack lived he would surely have been nominated. But now it is Lyndon Johnson who steps up.

It's August 1964, at the Democratic National Convention, and Bobby Kennedy has just introduced a film about Jack's all-too-short life. Remembering his brother, he says: "When I think of President Kennedy, I think of what Shakespeare said in Romeo and Juliet: 'When he shall die; Take him and cut him out in little stars; And he will make the face of heaven so fine; That all the world will be in love with the night; And pay no worship to the garish sun.'"

John F. Kennedy's gravesite at Arlington National Cemetery

chapter **11**

The Kennedy Legacy

In 1962, Teddy, the youngest Kennedy brother, makes a successful run for the Senate from the state of Massachusetts. The Kennedy brothers have hit the political hattrick. Jack is president, Bobby is attorney general, and Ted (born Edward) is the fresh young senator.

After Jack's death, Bobby thought he'd share the presidential ticket with Johnson in 1964, by becoming vice president, but Johnson does not pick Bobby. Bobby decides to run for senator from New York. He wins and, in 1967, decides to seek the Democratic nomination for president. Bobby symbolizes all the hopes and dreams that his brother could not fulfill.

Maybe Bobby could win the war on poverty or the war for equality between the races.

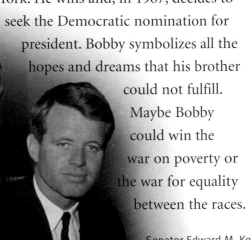

Senator Edward M. Kennedy and Attorney General Robert F. Kennedy announced the creation of the John F. Kennedy Library at a press conference on March 23, 1964.

Perhaps Bobby can end the war that is now raging in Vietnam. Maybe Bobby can pick up the pieces of the New Frontier.

But on a campaign stop in California, Bobby is shot and killed in the kitchen of a Los Angeles hotel. It is November 1963 all over again.

"Each time a man stands up for an ideal... he sends a tiny ripple of hope."

From Robert F. Kennedy's tombstone

Only a few months before Bobby is murdered, Dr. Martin Luther King, Jr., is assassinated. Three men of peace die before their time, and each would leave an enduring legacy of courage, hope, and dreams.

———————— • ————————

Ernest Hemingway said that there are no second acts in American lives. Jackie was about to prove him wrong.

Jackie and the children leave Washington for New York, a move that surprises many since she said that she would raise the president's children in the president's town. She buys an apartment at 1040 Fifth Avenue, overlooking the reservoir at Central Park, where she can often be spotted jogging around the path that circles the water.

After five years of being a widow, Jackie marries Greek shipping magnate Aristotle "Ari" Onassis in Greece. John and Caroline are there, as well as Jack's sisters Pat and Jean. Before marrying Onassis, Jackie had expressed that she was tired of being the Kennedy widow. The American public resents her remarrying, especially to this wealthy, much older man. She becomes Jackie O., a fixture on both the New York social and literary scenes.

Years before, Joe Kennedy had remarked that the way to sell magazines was to put Jack's picture on the cover. It's the same with Jackie. *Click.* She and Ari are photographed heading to P.J. Clarke's, a popular restaurant in Manhattan. *Click.* Jackie is photographed walking in pinstripe pants and a blazer. *Click. Click. Click.* She wins a legal case against a photographer, preventing him from getting too close to her family. During one encounter, Caroline actually kicked him.

There are pictures of Jackie, her head wrapped in a scarf, her dark eyes concealed behind oversized sunglasses, running from the photographers or confronting them head on.

Jackie's a New Yorker now. She becomes involved in landmark preservation. It is her testimony that saves Grand Central Station from the fate

On October 20, 1968, Jackie and Ari were married on Skorpios Island off the coast of Greece.

that befell the old Penn Station, which was torn down by people who thought having modern, convenient buildings was more important than history. Jackie brings the same reverence for history to this preservation project that she brought to the White House restoration.

After Onassis's death, Jackie becomes a book editor at Viking Publishers, and then at Doubleday, where she works until her death from cancer in 1994.

As adults, John and Caroline both go to law school in New York City. Caroline attends Columbia University and John, New York University.

John becomes one of New York's most eligible bachelors and becomes romantically linked with celebrities Daryl Hannah and Madonna. In 1988, *People* magazine names him the Sexiest Man Alive. After law school, when he fails the bar exam— the test to be certified to practice law—the *New York Post* declares THE HUNK FLUNKS. That same year he receives a standing ovation at the Democratic National Convention when he introduces his uncle, Ted Kennedy. After Jackie's death in 1994, John starts a magazine called *George* that focuses on the glamour of politics ("Not just politics as usual" is the motto). He was joining the two family interests, he said, publishing and politics.

On July 16, 1999, John, piloting his own plane from New York to Cape Cod to attend his cousin Rory's wedding, crashes into the Atlantic Ocean, killing himself, his wife of three years, Carolyn Bessette Kennedy, and her sister, Lauren Bessette.

Caroline marries Edwin Schlossberg, a museum and exhibit designer, in 1986. They have three children: Rose, born in 1988, Tatiana, born in 1990, and John, born in 1993.

Like her brother, Caroline gets involved with publishing. She is the author of *The Right to Privacy*, which was published in 1995. Her other books include *The Best-Loved Poems of Jacqueline Kennedy Onassis* (2001) and *Profiles in Courage for Our Time* (2002), a collection of essays that honor modern-day heroes.

Caroline now devotes her time to fundraising for New York City public schools.

———————— • ————————

Jack gave America his ideas, his beliefs, and ultimately, his life. He cared deeply about people.

John F. Kennedy, Jr., and Caroline Kennedy Schlossberg at their mother's funeral in New York, May 23, 1994.

He was a man who excelled at sports but could also recite poetry. Though he was the son of a rich man, he cared about employers paying a decent wage and improving conditions for the poor.

He woke America up from a post-World War II sleep and gave many people hope, a reason to excel, and an identity.

Thousands of young people flocked to Washington, D.C., to be a part of the New Frontier. People who believed in Jack's message and knew that it was better to do something for the country than to sit around and wait until the country did something for you.

He defrosted the Cold War and brought the country, if not the world, back from the brink of nuclear war.

Early in his administration he created the Peace Corps, sending young Americans all around the globe to help others.

Is There a Kennedy Curse?

The tragedies suffered by the Kennedy family have led people to believe in a Kennedy curse. Some say the bad luck began as long ago as 1858, when Patrick Kennedy, having left Ireland's potato famine for the U.S., died of cholera at age 35—exactly 105 years before J.F.K.'s death. During WWII, Jack's older brother Joe, considered the best and the brightest of the Kennedys, was killed in a plane explosion. Sister Kick died just four years later in another crash. Jack and Bobby's assassinations occurred within five years of each other. Most recently, Bobby's son, Michael Kennedy, was killed in Colorado when he skied backward into a tree while playing catch with family members. Then, in 1999, John Jr.'s plane went down, killing all on board and making people think the curse lives on.

Future president Bill
Clinton met President
John F. Kennedy in
1962 as part of the
American Legion's Boys
Nation program.

The nation and
the world mourned
when he died, but
out of those tears came
the desire to do better. Jack
influenced a lot of young people to do the right thing, to
go into politics, and to go out into the world and make it a
better place, whether by helping a developing country with
the Peace Corps, or by going into a poor neighborhood at
home and making a difference.

One young man from Arkansas visiting the White House
was particularly moved by his meeting with President Kennedy,
and one day, in the not too distant future, William Jefferson
Clinton would become a member of that exclusive club that
called 1600 Pennsylvania Avenue home.

He was a great man, but John F. Kennedy was human, too.
He suffered his whole life from overwhelming physical
ailments and diseases. He was often in pain and under the
care of many doctors. And recently revealed information has
shown that Jack was sicker than the American public knew,
that his poor health was kept from the nation.

"I ask for your help and your prayers, as I embark on this new and solemn journey."

John F. Kennedy, January 9, 1961, just before taking office, in a Boston farewell speech

As with all modern presidents, his errors were played out in the press and in the public arena. Poor decisions about the Bay of Pigs invasion almost cost him his reputation. And many think he and his administration didn't do enough to support the civil rights movement.

Yet despite the obstacles and shortcomings, John F. Kennedy and his nearly thousand days in office are remembered by most as a beacon of light that brought positive change to our country.

After his death, Jackie said that Jack's White House was like Camelot, that legendary place of ideals and dreams that Jack first read about as a boy. His administration is remembered for its energy, excitement, and possibility. Today Jack's vision lives on.

Selected Words of President John F. Kennedy

"The path we have chosen for the present is full of hazards, as all paths are—but it is the one most consistent with our character and courage as a nation and our commitments around the world. The cost of freedom is always high—and Americans have always paid it. And one path we shall never choose, and that is the path of surrender or submission.

"Our goal is not the victory of might, but the vindication of right—not peace at the expense of freedom, but both peace and freedom, here in this hemisphere, and, we hope, around the world. God willing, that goal will be achieved."

—Radio and Television Report to the American People on the Soviet Arms Buildup in Cuba, October 22, 1962

J.F.K.'s Press Conferences

While Joe Sr. understood Hollywood and movies, Jack was the first politician to understand and use the new medium of television. It was a natural partnership. Jack held frequent press conferences that were televised around the nation and became popular viewing because of his wit, spontaneity, and intelligence. In his nearly thousand days in office, he held 64 such conferences, transcripts of which can be found on the Kennedy Library Web site.

"One hundred years of delay have passed since President Lincoln freed the slaves, yet their heirs, their grandsons, are not fully free. They are not yet freed from the bonds of injustice, they are not yet freed from social and economic oppression. And this nation, for all its hopes and all its boasts, will not be fully free until all its citizens are free."

—JFK speaks to the nation on TV about the civil rights bill he is sending to Congress, June 11, 1963

"We in this country, in this generation, are—by destiny rather than choice—the watchmen on the walls of world freedom. We ask, therefore, that we may be worthy of our power and responsibility, that we may exercise our strength with wisdom and restraint, and that we may achieve in our time and for all time the ancient vision of 'peace on earth, good will toward men.'"

—Remarks prepared for delivery at the Trade Mart in Dallas, November 22, 1963

Events in the Life of John F. Kennedy

MAY 29, 1917
John Fitzgerald Kennedy
is born in Brookline,
Massachusetts.

NOVEMBER 4, 1952
Kennedy is elected
senator from
Massachusetts.

NOVEMBER 25, 1960
John Fitzgerald
Kennedy, Jr. is born.

FEBRUARY 20, 1920
Jack contracts
scarlet fever.

NOVEMBER 27, 1957
Caroline Bouvier
Kennedy is born.

NOVEMBER 8, 1960
John F. Kennedy is
elected president of
the United States.

1917

NOVEMBER 5, 1946
Kennedy is elected
to his first of three
terms in Congress.

1954–1955
Kennedy has two
operations on his back.

APRIL–AUGUST 1943
Jack serves as captain of
PT-109 in the U.S. Navy
during World War II.

SEPTEMBER 12, 1953
Kennedy marries Jacqueline
Bouvier, who is twelve
years younger than he.

JANUARY 20, 1961
The inauguration
of John F. Kennedy

NOVEMBER 22, 1963
John F. Kennedy is
assassinated in Dallas.

JULY 16, 1999
John Jr. dies in a plane
crash with his wife and
his sister-in-law.

MAY 25, 1961
Kennedy gives speech in which he
establishes the goal of landing
U.S. astronauts on the moon.

OCTOBER 1979
The Kennedy Library
is dedicated in
Boston,
Massachusetts.

1999

OCTOBER 16–28, 1962
Cuban Missile Crisis

MAY 19, 1994
Jacqueline Bouvier
Kennedy Onassis dies
of cancer in New York.

APRIL 17, 1961
Bay of Pigs
Invasion in
Cuba

JUNE 26, 1963
Kennedy gives speech
at Berlin Wall.

NOVEMBER 25, 1963
John F. Kennedy's
funeral and interment

123

Bibliography

Anderson, Catherine Corley. *John F. Kennedy, Young People's President.* Minneapolis: Lerner Publication Co., 1991.

Cooper, Ilene. *Jack: The Early Years of John F. Kennedy.* New York: Dutton Children's Books, 2003.

Dallek, Robert. *An Unfinished Life: John F. Kennedy (1917–1963).* Boston: Little, Brown and Company, 2003.

Gogerly, Liz. *Days That Shook the World: The Kennedy Assassination, November 22, 1963.* Austin: Raintree Steck-Vaughn Publishers, 2003.

Goodwin, Doris Kearns. *The Fitzgeralds and the Kennedys: An American Saga.* New York: Simon and Schuster, 1987.

Hersey, John. *Of Men and War.* New York: Scholastic Book Services, 1963.

Jones, Rebecca C. *The President Has Been Shot: True Stories of the Attacks on Ten U.S. Presidents.* New York: Dutton Children's Books, 1996.

Kennedy, Rose Fitzgerald. *Times to Remember.* New York: Doubleday & Co., 1974.

Manchester, William. *One Brief Shining Moment: Remembering Kennedy.* Boston and Toronto: Little, Brown and Company, 1983.

Schroeder, Alan. *Forty Years of High Risk Television.* New York: Columbia University Press, 2000.

Smith, Amanda, ed. *Hostage to Fortune: The Letters of Joseph P. Kennedy.* New York: Viking, 2001.

Thomas, Evan. *Robert Kennedy: His Life.* New York: Simon and Schuster, 2000.

The Warren Commission Report on the Assassination of John F. Kennedy, originally published 1964.

White, Theodore H. *The Making of the President, 1960.* New York: Atheneum, 1988.

Sources Cited

Page 9: Dr. Edwin Place: *The Fitzgeralds and the Kennedys,* p. 310; Quotes: *Times to Remember;* The sum of the donation, $3,700, is from *Times to Remember,* p. 310, and *The Fitzgeralds and the Kennedys.*

Page 10: Mosquito joke: www.jfklibrary.org; Newspaper articles on the Irish potato famine: vassun.vassar.edu/~sttaylor/FAMINE/ILN/PotatoDisease.html; Statistics on deaths and coffin ships: www.people.virginia.edu/~eas5e/Irish/Famine.html; 1,186,000 Irish immigrants: *One Brief Shining Moment.*

Page 12: Family history: *Times to Remember.*

Page 18: Rose Kennedy talks about Kennedy's love of reading and talks of his weaving daydreams: *Times to Remember.*

Page 21: Family trips to Boston Harbor: *John F. Kennedy, Young People's President.*

Page 22: Rose recounts the differences between her two oldest sons: *Times to Remember,* p. 118.

Page 23: Disciplining children: *Times to Remember,* p. 132.

Page 25: Reciting passage from St. Luke: *Times to Remember,* p. 388; Family outings: *Times to Remember,* p. 99.

Page 27: Rose describes her children greeting their father at the train station: *Times to Remember,* p. 86.

Page 28: The Devotion School: http://devotion.brookline.mec.edu/ and phone interview with principal on January 2, 2004; Dexter: *The Fitzgeralds and the Kennedys;* Dexter uniform description: *Jack: The Early Years;* Rose and public schools: *The Fitzgeralds and the Kennedys,* p. 457; Kennedy's comments when teacher is due: *Times to Remember,* p. 97.

Page 31: Quote from Kennedy to his father: *Hostage to Fortune;* Letter from Joe Sr. to Kennedy about clothes pressing: *Hostage to Fortune;* "having the goods": *Hostage to Fortune.*

Page 33: Kennedy's weight and physical ailments: *Times to Remember,* p. 176.

Page 36: Kennedy's trying to make the varsity swim team and having his roommate Torbert Macdonald sneak food into the infirmary: *Times to Remember,* p. 215; "Room 32 of Whedon Hall": *The Fitzgeralds and the Kennedys,* p. 504.

Page 43: Joe Sr. helps with Kennedy's naval physical form: *The Fitzgeralds and the Kennedys,* p. 627.

Page 44: Quote from Kennedy's phrase book: *One Brief Shining Moment,* p. 33; "This is how it feels to die": *Of Men and War.*

Page 45: Information on PT boats and *PT-109:* www.history.navy.mil/faqs/faq60-5.htm; coconut text: news.nationalgeographic.com/news/2002/07/0709_020710_kennedyPT109.html.

Page 46: "involuntary hero:" *Times to Remember;* More on the 2002 discovery of *PT-109:* news.nationalgeographic.com/news/2002/05/0529_020529_ballard.html#related.

Page 47: Statistics on Joe Jr.'s deadly mission: *The Fitzgeralds and the Kennedys,* p. 662.

Page 50: Kennedy's words to Dave Powers appear in various biographies of the president and the JFK Library website: www.jfklibrary.org/dave_powers/html; Powers's description of meeting young Kennedy: *Times to Remember.*

Page 52: Kennedy in clothes: *An Unfinished Life*; Kennedy's senatorial campaign issues: *An Unfinished Life*.

Page 53: Lodge's tea party comments: *Times to Remember*, p. 326; Election night returns: *One Brief Shining Moment*, p. 63.

Page 54: Queen Deb: *One Brief Shining Moment*, p. 65; Wedding details: *Times to Remember*, p. 350.

Page 58: The country in 1958: *An Unfinished Life*, p. 236.

Page 59: Kennedy's 1958 article: *An Unfinished Life*, p. 289.

Page 65: Jackie in supermarket: *Times to Remember*, p. 366.

Page 66: Kennedy's big win in Wisconsin: *Times to Remember*, p. 367.

Page 67: "Happy Days Are Here Again": *One Brief Shining Moment*, p. 113.

Page 68: Sidebar information: www.commondreams.org/views/081300-105.htm; New Frontier speech: www.jfklibrary.org/j071560.htm.

Page 71: Information about Nixon and Checkers: www.watergate.info/nixon/checkers-speech.html; Difference in style between Kennedy and Nixon: *The Making of the President*, p. 65.

Page 72: Background on first Chicago debate: *Presidential Debates*.

Page 73: Radio audience thought Nixon won first debate: *An Unfinished Life*, p. 286; Kennedy like a young Lincoln: *Times to Remember*, p. 374; Miles aboard the *Caroline*: *John F. Kennedy, Young People's President*, p. 69.

Page 74: Economics of late 1950s–1960: *An Unfinished Life*, p. 309.

Page 76: Election night statistics: *One Brief Shining Moment*, p. 121; Duration of speech: *Times to Remember*, p. 390.

Page 78: Transcript of Kennedy's speech: www.jfklibrary.org/60-1st.htm; "poets and politics": *An Unfinished Life*, p. 203; Retrieving Fitzgerald family Bible: *Times to Remember*, p. 386.

Page 82: Particulars of Oval Office: *One Brief Shining Moment*, p. 138.

Page 83: Kennedy establishes the Peace Corps: www.jfklibrary.org/jfk_peace_corps.html.

Page 88: Freedom Riders: americanhistory.si.edu/onthemove/collection/object_546.html.

Page 90: Kennedy and the moon: www.jfklibrary.org/j052561.htm; Information on conversation with Webb: www.jfklibrary.org/pr_jfk_tapes_tape63.html.

Page 92: Southern hemisphere challenges: www.jfklibrary.org/j052561.htm.

Page 95 "a cold winter": *Robert Kennedy*, p. 136; Eight ways to get rid of Fidel Castro: *Robert Kennedy*, p. 152; Khrushchev and DeGaulle, Gary Powers: americanhistory.about.com/library/weekly/aa061801a.htm.

Page 97: Kennedy addresses the nation, October 22, 1962: www.jfklibrary.org/j102262.htm; Reconnaissance plane: *One Brief Shining Moment*, p. 201.

Page 98: Information on the day-to-day events in the White House: www.gwu.edu/~nsarchiv/nsa/cuba_mis_cri/audio.htm.

Page 101: Poster from San Antonio: *John F. Kennedy, Young People's President*, p. 126.

Page 102: Time sequence of Kennedy's assassination: *Days That Shook the World*; Lincoln facts: *The President Has Been Shot*.

Page 105: "Everybody will know…": *The Warren Commission Report on the Assassination of John F. Kennedy*.

Page 106: "I am certain…": kennedy-center.org/about/history.html

Page 108: Features of riderless horse and caisson: *John F. Kennedy, Young People's President*, p. 133.

Page 109: Nellie Connally's quote from her notes. Interview with Larry King, July 4, 2002: www.cnn.com/TRANSCRIPTS/0207/04/lkl.00.html

Page 111: Robert Kennedy's speech: www.jfklibrary.org/r082764.htm.

For Further Study

Plan a trip to Boston to visit the **John F. Kennedy National Historic Site**—Kennedy's birthplace and boyhood home located at 83 Beale Street—and the John F. Kennedy Library and Museum on Columbia Point. While in Boston, you can also explore the many historic places Kennedy saw as a child.

If you are unable to take a trip to Boston, you can learn more about the John F. Kennedy Library and Museum at **www.jfklibrary.org**

More on the 2002 discovery of *PT-109* at **nationalgeographic.com/pt109**

For information on the United States Senate, check out this government Web site: **www.senate.gov/reference/reference_index_subjects/Senators_vrd.htm**

New York University has an interesting site about Alger Hiss and McCarthyism: **homepages.nyu.edu/~th15/history.html**

The Smithsonian Web site about the Freedom Riders has images of a burning Freedom Rider bus and information about the segregated bus system: **americanhistory.si.edu/onthemove/collection/object_546.html**

KENNEDY IS SHOT, REPORTED DEAD

Index

Author's Note

I wish to acknowledge the John Fitzgerald Kennedy Library for granting generous permission to quote from the speeches of President Kennedy. Thanks go to the terrific staff at DK, including, Madeline Farbman, Dirk Kaufman, Gregor Hall, Crissie Johnson, Laaren Brown, Lenny Hort, and especially editor Beth Sutinis, to whom I'm grateful. Thanks, too, to Gail Spilsbury, Katy Woerner, John Blee, Tashi, and the gang at home.

DK Publishing, Inc., wishes to give special thanks to James B. Hill of the John Fitzgerald Kennedy Library for his kind and speedy help in researching photographs.

Picture Credits

The publisher would like to thank the following for their kind permission to reproduce the following photographs: (t=top; b=bottom; l=left; r=right; c=center; a=above) Courtesy John Fitzgerald Kennedy Library, Boston: 1; ©Corbis: 2–3, 4, 5; ©Bettmann/Corbis: 6–7; ©Corbis: 8, 11; ©Bettmann/Corbis: 12; ©Corbis: 14; Courtesy John Fitzgerald Kennedy Library, Boston: 16, 16–17; Courtesy of the National Park Service, John F. Kennedy National Historic Site/Perron: 17; Courtesy John Fitzgerald Kennedy Library, Boston: 18; Kennedy Family Collection, John Fitzgerald Kennedy Library, Boston: 20; ©Bettmann/Corbis: 21; ©Todd A. Gipstein/Corbis: 22; Courtesy John Fitzgerald Kennedy Library, Boston: 24, 25, 26–27; ©Bettmann/Corbis: 29t, 29b; Courtesy John Fitzgerald Kennedy Library, Boston: 31; ©Bettmann/Corbis: 32–33; ©Corbis: 34; ©Phil Schermeister/Corbis: 35; ©Hulton Archive/Getty Images: 36; ©Hulton-Deutsch Collection/Corbis: 37; ©Hulton Archive/Getty Images: 38; DK Cartography Department, London: 39; ©Bettmann/Corbis: 40; ©Hulton Archive/Getty Images: 41; ©Bettmann/Corbis: 42; ©Hulton Archive/Getty Images: 43; Courtesy John Fitzgerald Kennedy Library, Boston: 44; ©Bettmann/Corbis: 45t; ©AP Wide World: 45b; Courtesy John Fitzgerald Kennedy Library, Boston: 46t; Courtesy John Fitzgerald Kennedy Library, Boston: 46b; ©Bettmann/Corbis: 47t, 47b, 48, 49; Courtesy John Fitzgerald Kennedy Library, Boston: 50; ©Time Life Pictures/Getty Images: 52; ©AP Wide World: 54; ©Corbis: 55; ©Bettmann/Corbis: 57, 58–59; ©Corbis: 61; ©Bettmann/Corbis: 62, 63; ©AP Wide World: 65; ©Richard Cummins/Corbis: 66; ©Bettmann/Corbis: 68, 69; ©David J. & Janice L. Frent Collection/Corbis: 70; ©Bettmann/Corbis: 71; ©Corbis: 72–73; ©Bettmann/Corbis: 74–75; ©David J. & Janice L. Frent Collection/Corbis: 76; ©Bettmann/Corbis: 77, 78; ©Time Life Pictures/Getty Images: 79; ©Bettmann/Corbis: 80, 81, 82, 84; ©AP Wide World: 86–87; ©Bettmann/Corbis: 88; ©Time Life Pictures/Getty Images: 89; ©NASA/Roger Ressmeyer/Corbis: 90; ©Dean Conger/Corbis: 91; ©Bettmann/Corbis: 92; ©AFP/Corbis: 93t; ©Bettmann/Corbis: 93b; ©Corbis: 94; ©Bettmann/Corbis: 95t, 95b, 96, 98; ©Reuters/Corbis: 99; ©Bettmann/Corbis: 100, 103; ©Hulton Archive/Getty Images: 104t; ©Bettmann/Corbis: 104b; ©AP Wide World: 105; ©Wally McNamee/Corbis: 106–107; ©Hulton Archive/Getty Images: 107; ©Corbis: 108; ©Royalty-Free/Corbis: 111; ©Bettmann/Corbis: 112, 114–115; ©Reuters/Corbis: 116; ©Corbis: 118; ©Bettmann/Corbis: 119, 120, 124–125, 126–127.

Border photos, from left to right ©Bettmann; Stanley Tretick, 1963/Corbis: a; ©AP Wide World: b; ©Royalty-Free/Corbis: c; ©Hulton Archive/Getty Images: d; ©Bettmann/Corbis: e; ©Corbis: f; ©Bettmann/Corbis: g, h, i, j; ©Richard Cummins/Corbis: k; Courtesy John Fitzgerald Kennedy Library, Boston: l; ©Bettmann/Corbis: m.